17.20

D0198665

3 1215 00091 8604

I ASKED FOR INTIMACY

ALSO BY RENITA J. WEEMS

Just a Sister Away:
A Womanist Vision of Women's Relationships in the Bible

I Asked for Intimacy

Stories of Blessings, Betrayals, and Birthings

R E N I T A   J .   W E E M S

San Diego, California

LuraMedia™

LuraMedia
7060 Miramar Road, Suite 104
San Diego, CA 92121

Library of Congress Cataloging-in-Publication Data
  Weems, Renita, date.
      I asked for intimacy : stories of blessings, betrayals, and birthings /
  Renita J. Weems.
        p.   cm.
      Includes bibliographical references.
      ISBN 0-931055-80-6
      1. Interpersonal relations. 2. Intimacy (Psychology).
    3. Women–Religious life. 4. Religious life–Christianity.
    5. Weems, Renita J., date.   I. Title.
    HM132.W363   1993   93-13730
    158.2–dc20   CIP

Portions of this book have appeared earlier in somewhat different form in *Essence* and *Sage* magazines:

"Hush. Mama's Gotta Go Bye-Bye" was originally published by *Sage* magazine under the same title and by *Essence* magazine as "This Mother's Daughter."

"When Love Hurts" was originally published by *Essence* magazine.

"Just Friends" was originally published by *Essence* magazine.

An earlier version of "Daddy's Girl" was first written for *Essence* magazine, which will publish it in a future issue.

The Scripture translations are the author's own from the Hebrew and Greek Bibles.

*Because this book was completed the day before her birth,
I dedicate it to Savannah Nia Weems Espinosa, my first born,
whom I am convinced my mother sent from heaven
to bless me and to help erase from my memory
the years of my mother's betrayal.*

Mama, I dis-remember. Thank you.

Contents

Preface

Writing provides me the medium to ask the questions I am too embarrassed or too afraid to ask aloud. For example, I've always wanted to ask God why children die, why women stay in abusive relationships, why it is easier sometimes to hate than to love, why my mother was an alcoholic and, in as much as I'm a minister, why God won't once and for all rid me of my demons. These are, for me, intimate questions, and they lay at the basis of what to me it means to live a life of faith. It seems that I have been on a search all my life for faith in intimate places. And the most intimate of places, as far as I am concerned, is in the area of human relationships, relationships between men and women, women and women, women and children, men and women and God and so on. Which is why *I ASKED FOR INTIMACY*, like my earlier book, *JUST A SISTER AWAY*, is an exploration of intimate relationships, mothers and daughters, mothers and sons, daughters and fathers, and women's friendships. I suppose you can say that everything I know about God I have learned in the muck of intimate human interchange.

I ASKED FOR INTIMACY records where my searches for faith have sometimes taken me.

One of the reasons I first began writing was because I found myself chafing under my conservative, fundamentalist, evangelical upbringing. I needed a medium in which to raise forbidden questions. I thought my Christian training would provide me a framework for tackling the issues facing my hyphenated life as an African-American Christian woman. But that was not always the case. I couldn't believe that life was as simplistic, predictable, and censorious as my narrow religious upbringing insisted. Instead of teaching me how to think and work through my relationships, my religion helped to mask my insecurities behind a veil of petrified sanctimony. Writing about how relationships are affected by ambition, violence, addictions, sexuality, and health has sometimes led me as a Christian to unorthodox conclusions. And that's all right. Because in the process I've found lasting relationships.

Earlier versions of some of the chapters in this book were previously published in other publications. Revising them and bringing them together here have forced me to sharpen my thinking on many topics. It has also let me see the stream of braid that winds its way throughout my writings that has to do with a woman's quest for intimacy, connectedness, and wholeness. In that regard, *I ASKED FOR INTIMACY* continues the conversation that I began in *JUST A SISTER AWAY*. In both I explore women's passions, fears, celebrations, and contradictions. The difference between the two books is that whereas before I relied upon Scripture's stories about women to help me unravel women's experience, this time in *I ASKED FOR INTIMACY* I allow my own experience as an African-American woman to help me in some places interrogate Scripture and in other places reconceive what faith is. Some readers may be disappointed that the Bible study format, namely the presence of questions at the end of each chapter, has been abandoned in this book. I hope, however, that the contents will inspire readers to find and ask their own questions in light of their own realities.

I have written this book trying to bring together and tap into the best of my multiple, hyphenated identities: writer, biblical scholar, Christian, woman, and African-American. I've tried to combine my talents as a writer with my discipline as a scholar and my hope as a Christian, along with my perspective as a woman and my gift for storytelling as an African-American, to write with about very complicated, intimate matters with integrity, imagination, and verve.

Too few books from the perspective of African-American Christian women have been written. When there are more, perhaps I will not have to write with African-American Christian women in mind. But in the meantime, I do. That is not to exclude other readers, rather it identifies whose ear I imagined myself whispering in as I wrote this book. I didn't imagine whispering in *any* one's ear, nor in *every*one's ear. I saw myself leaning over to my sisters' ears, reaching for idioms and symbols that would engage their imagination. I wanted to whisper hope in the ears of African-American women because in our patriarchal culture we seem always to be on a most desperate search to be loved, to be accepted, to be discussed, to be known for who we really are.

Finally, because writers live in relationships with other people, or ought to, no book is the work of a single author. Every author needs support groups. Female authors need them more. A special thanks goes to my publisher, Lura Jane Geiger, and my editor, Marcia Broucek, who patiently midwifed me through the writing. And because *I ASKED FOR INTIMACY* is the result of many conversations and dialogues that took place at women's retreats and workshops across the country, from New York to Washington, D.C., from San Antonio to Detroit, I want to acknowledge the challenges and insights that I gained from those women. I've even taken their advice when they told me in so many words to stop hiding behind what the Bible says and tell them what I really think.

And, finally, I want to thank my husband, Martin L. Espinosa, who learned from this book what it means to be married to a writer. That is, every intimacy is seed to a writer, and the best writing is often done after midnight. It is just a shame that he had to learn all of this in the first year of our marriage. Our daughter, Savannah Nia, has probably been the most patient through this entire process of writing. It has competed for her mother's attention the first three months of her life. Every night after midnight she has waited patiently for me to be done with my writing so that I might walk her twelve times around the dining room table in the dark and sing to her until she is exhausted with sleep. Even now as I type these closing lines with one hand, my daughter nurses quietly at my breast. She is teaching me the most about intimacy and faith. She smiles at me even though I am staring at my computer, she coos back when I talk to myself, and she rubs her hand across my face when I am engrossed with my next paragraph. She has come to offer me what I have longed for most. Intimacy.

I ASKED FOR INTIMACY

Letter to an Unborn Child

I have been journaling now for more than fifteen years. It began as a way to talk to myself while at work without calling attention to myself. I hated my job, and I didn't have anyone to tell. Every day at break time and during lunch, I would pour out my frustrations, my ambitions, and my passions onto scraps of paper that I tucked in my brief case, my Evan Picone suit pocket and, once, even in my bosom. It was about that time that I also decided to become a writer. The ambition to become a writer, I decided, meant that I would never have children. I don't remember being saddened by the thought. In fact, I wrote in my journal a eulogy to that part of me that would never be born.

Looking over those journal entries fifteen years later, I am taken by how dire was my every impulse. Every longing was desperate. Every ambition was consuming. Every failure was damning. Every relationship was filled with melodrama.

I am glad now that I have a transcript of those years. It's good to be able to see how very much, in fifteen years, my life has changed in some respects, and how much it has not changed, in others. It's especially revealing to see that, with time, girls filled with questions mature into women ripened by more eloquent questions — and their own contradictions.

I asked for intimacy. And in an imagined conversation with an unborn child, I obtained a glimpse of eternity instead.

_____
_____

*In the midst of wavering between indecision and conviction,
I seize this one lucid moment to explain to you the things
that are going through my mind as I contemplate motherhood. Although at the time of this writing, my decision has
not been made, I may very well decide against ever having
a child. That being the decision, I thought you deserved an
explanation. You deserve to know why I may decide not to
have you — not conceive you, not carry you, not birth you,
not know what it is to love a child. I pray that you won't
think harshly of me and will find it in your heart to hear my
side of the story. It's not often that women like me who elect
to remain barren are heard. I just thought you might like to
know that I have my reasons . . .*

This week marks my ninth month of pregnancy. The hysteria
has abated, only to be replaced by a feeling of powerlessness. My body
doesn't belong to me anymore. Every morning I awaken to find that, little
by little, my pot belly has grown to be a full-fledged tub of flesh. (Amazing
how three years of working out and stomach toning are totally wiped out
by one night of passion.) I look like a government mule. A pregnant
woman has no privacy. Perfect strangers come up to me and offer that I
must be having twins. I stare and snarl. "So when is your baby due?" the
bagger at the grocery, the exterminator, and the postman inquire. I don't
remember these people talking to me before when I wasn't pregnant. "It
doesn't matter when it's due," I want to shout, "you won't be there."
Instead, I smile and answer. Pregnancy has evidently compromised my
power to intimidate.

When the baby comes, what in the world will I do with this surplus of flesh around my waist? It took me three years of exercise to find the waistline I've lost to pregnancy. I don't have another three years of energy to devote to this matter. And what in the world happened to my hair? I've never had hair so dry. Although friends who've gone through this dole out helpful advice, warnings, and speculations, I miss not having my mother to steady me through my pregnancy and assuage my fears. Never in the eight years since her death have I dreamed as much about her as I do now. The other night I dreamed she showed me her womb. We look so much alike, my mother and I. We are built the same, we have the same walk and the same laughter. This makes her about the only person whose advice I can trust right now. But she's dead, and the most I remember about my mother as she carried my three younger siblings was that she was radiant. (When I'm told that I'm radiant pregnant, I smile politely and remember the acne that has plagued me since my teens, thinking to myself, "Hmmph that's just the oil in my skin that can't make a decent pimple right now.") Pregnant and numb, dazed and reclusive, I stumble through these months without a mother to relieve my every curiosity, like whether it's normal for Baker (my mother's maiden name) women to grow hair under their chins when they're pregnant or whether fibroids are common among the women in our family.

Let me begin by saying that there are those who will think me foolish to worry about you. As far as they are concerned, since you haven't even been conceived, you're not real. But you are a real possibility. For I know that every time I lie down in intimacy, I run the chance of rising up pregnant. So it's just a matter of time. Tonight I want to reckon with your possibility, though not your inevitability. You know, the thought of having a baby was once ridiculous to me. But in the course of time, you have evolved from ridiculous to unlikely, to not sure, to possibly, to today a decision that must be made. I am proud of you. You're a survivor.

A few nights into my fifth month of pregnancy, I lay on the floor of my study waiting for my husband to come upstairs to help me back up on my feet. Surrounded by old journals and journal entries sprawled around my legs, I came upon a journal entry dated 1978. I recognized the type from my old college Remington typewriter. (I bought that typewriter with my earnings from a job at Dairy Queen.) Having quit my job on Wall Street in 1978 and taken up residence in New York as a starving, unemployed poet, I was just beginning to dream about becoming a writer, a thinker, a critic. A woman with a mind of her own. Judging by the contents of that 1978 journal entry, I was also beginning to count the cost of my ambitions. One of the costs, I imagined, was that I would probably never have children. Which was probably my way of saying that I'd probably never get married. I remember feeling relieved by the decision. I was afraid of duplicating myself.

Babies had never really fascinated me, and men were people I agreed to go out with when the month was longer than my unemployment check. In my-then-typical melodramatic and overwrought manner, I thought I should mark my decision not to have a baby by writing a letter to "my baby," explaining my reasons. I hadn't read that letter since I'd written it. Strange that I should happen upon the letter to my unborn child these many years later when I'm five months pregnant.

The truth is I'm afraid to be a mother. Though the fourth of twelve children (including stepsisters and brothers), I understand very little about what it means to be a mother. What I think I know more about are the pains, heartaches, and disappointments of motherhood. At least that's what I imagine drove my mother to abandon her children.

I think, why press my luck. I probably wouldn't make a good mother anyway. I couldn't: I have no natural inclinations for the job. I'm one of those women who never ask to hold the baby. No matter how cute and gurgly, no matter how much they coo and smile at me, I never think to reach for them. They may be adorable, but I've never met one that was irresistible. Still, it isn't that I don't like children. I do. At least some, anyway. I simply don't have any example of healthy parents, nor healthy parenting. After all, love is rarely any better than the lover: sick people love sickly, and frightened people, like myself, live in fear of love. I'm afraid to love you.

Everyone thinks that, because of my age and because I've only been married thirteen months, this pregnancy was planned, that I was trying to beat the biological clock. Nothing could be further from the truth. I was certain I was unable to conceive, surely unable to carry a child to term. Never mind that I'd used contraceptives all my adult life; still, I had talked myself into believing that I was infertile. And I was happy childless. So when my husband suggested that we try — and I agreed, thinking that (in the outside event that I wasn't infertile) it would take me at least six months to even conceive the fetus, which I would eventually miscarry within the first ten weeks — imagine my horror when I found out I was pregnant after the first month of "trying." Between two manuscripts overdue at the publishers, scores of upcoming speaking engagements, fall classes beginning in a couple of months, helping out at my husband's church, a busted toilet, a slow draining bathtub, ferns and other plants dying to be replanted, arguments with my husband about the checks I forget to record, when in the world would I have time and where in my life was I going to put a baby? I liked, and had grown accustomed to, living in fourth gear.

> *I'm not sure if I'm ready to give up my dreams in exchange for diapers, rattlers, and drool. Just the thought of staying up all night with a colicky baby makes me chew on my blouse. There are so many things I want to do. Today I want to write. Tomorrow I want to write. Ten years from now I want to be found writing. Many of the most tragic women I know, my mother being the best example, are those whose only crime is not having too many babies, but having too few dreams. I don't want to live like that.*

> *If what I really need is to be loved, I don't think it's a child's love that I need most. I don't want to have a child so as to have someone to love me. It may well be that I am not lovable.*

> *I don't want to have a child so I will have someone to take care of me when I grow old. I hope to have a pension plan by then.*

> *I don't need an extension of myself. Not everyone should reproduce themselves.*

> *Nor am I interested in leaving my signature upon history in the form of a child. I could be very happy just being remembered as a footnote.*

I am blessed to be surrounded by some very special friends who stand with me through my erratic moments of happiness and coax me through the times when I'm bewildered. But five months of pregnancy has taught me most keenly how to steer clear of my detractors. They're the ones who gloat at my being pregnant – not out of happiness for me, but in delight, knowing that at last I shall become like them: immobile, frustrated, stuck, self-sacrificing, unappreciated, and forever dog-tired.

"YOU pregnant?!" they invariably ask with unrestrained smugness.

"Finally, you'll know what it is to be a woman," I hear in their tone.

On the whole, the detractors fall into two camps: First are the married acquaintances who evidently envied my being single. They are now disappointed in me and resent that I've robbed them of the vicarious pleasure of living through my independence and mobility. Second are my single acquaintances. They find my pregnancy (and marriage), at best, an encroachment upon our previous life together and, at worst, a painful reminder of their own feelings of emptiness.

I guess what I'm trying to say is that my circle of friends has severely narrowed since becoming pregnant. The only people I talk to these days are those who love me and accept my contradictions.

Most people's shock over my pregnancy is second only to their astonishment that I finally married. Or, more accurately, their amazement that someone was intrepid enough to marry me.

"Did you think I was lesbian?" I invariably ask. That always leaves them silent.

"What kind of man married a woman as strong, educated, and accomplished as yourself?" a college friend once asked. The inference being men prefer weak, dense, failures like her (who, by the way, was on her second marriage). I wondered whether she heard herself.

"Well, it looks as though you're doing all the things you said you wouldn't do," another friend commented. I don't remember telling *her* that I didn't plan to marry or have a children. I don't believe I've ever articulated those words to anyone. Most people just assumed that I wouldn't.

> *Can you forgive me if I tell you that there are times when I resent your crowding into my mental space. And if that weren't enough, you force me to contemplate who your father might be. All these years I've been content living single. What's wrong with being single? I don't know anyone who is married who I'd trade places with. "Why have sex with a man you wouldn't want to have a baby by?" a sanctimonious friend of mine once queried. One has nothing to do with the other, I think. Married, with two children, she evidently is still having sex with a man she wants no more children by. Besides I'm not a cow; just because I can breed doesn't mean I ought to breed.*

Besides the changes in my body, there have been some major changes in my psychological and emotional states since becoming pregnant. I've become a recluse. I've not been this withdrawn from social contact since I was a teen-ager. But I'm not depressed . . . that's not true. I'm not *as* depressed now as I was during the first three months of pregnancy. I think I've come to grips with being pregnant. There are even moments when I look forward to having a baby. And I can't think of a better man I would want to have a baby with. He lotions the legs I can no longer find. He lies and says he still finds me sexy. Yes, I think I've made my peace with pregnancy, as much as that's possible.

All I do these days is write, take long baths, and suck on Popsicles. I rarely answer the telephone, and I make myself go to church on Sundays so as not to offend God. (It's better to stay on speaking terms with God, I rationalize; I just may need a little grace during delivery.) I try to read the Bible, but I am only exasperated by its profoundly male point of view. Strange, but while I've always been aware that the Bible was written from a male perspective and that it presumes its audience to be male also — I've certainly written and spoken about its male-centered viewpoint — I've never felt so estranged from its interests as I do now in pregnancy. I find nothing captivating about rivalries between barren and fertile women (Sarah and Hagar, Rachel and Leah). I fail to see the justice in sentencing a woman to the inexorable pain of childbirth on account of eating an apple (the story of Eve). I find no solace in virginal births (the story of Mary). And I fail to see the connection between my world and that of women whose sole ambition seems to be to bear children, preferably male (virtually every woman in the Bible). Surely these women are the product of the vain imaginations of men. I need in the Bible a woman I can recognize, one who is as aggrieved by pregnancy as she is elated, as fascinated by her sexuality as she is frightened by it, and as dissatisfied with her life as she is proud of it. I close the Bible, and I search for God in other ways.

I write letters to God. I write letters to friends. I write to myself.

Pregnancy forces me to write in a more urgent fashion these days in my journal. I write as a way of inventing my own stories and as a way of inventing myself. (I often say that I keep a journal to stay on speaking terms with the many women who live inside me.) But before I can write, I must first read. I find myself reading my old journal entries over and over. I pour through them, perhaps in a desperate attempt to reacquaint myself with a part of me that I fear is dying. With the birth of this baby, I am afraid that I am about to lose someone special inside. I'm afraid to let her go. I'm afraid I'll never see her again. "What you will gain will be more than what you will lose," says a friend. But I am not convinced.

The day my menstrual period began when I was twelve years old, you were trying to prepare me for you. And the first night I lay with a man, you whispered in my ear that it was just a matter of time now.

Skimming through journal pages, I recall old love affairs, past ambitions, former worries, nagging insecurities, old passions, unanswered prayers, outlived fears, past vexations. And I wonder when I grew beyond these obsessions. I don't remember. But one day I did. While my memory of them is still palpable, somehow and somewhere they lost their urgency. They've been replaced with new ambitions, new worries, new insecurities, new passions, new fears, and new vexations. With a baby on the way, everything takes on a different meaning.

You exist whether I choose to give birth to you or not. And the reality of your presence has nothing to do with whether or not I believe in abortion. You exist. You exist because I exist. And not even this letter to you explaining myself, justifying myself, can negate you. You are the child who lives inside me whether I bear you or not.

My baby is due in two weeks. Strange . . . for the longest time I would not refer to it as a baby. For the first three months, I said "fetus." Even during the eleventh week when I bled for three days straight and was doubled over in pain and prayed that I wouldn't lose it, I still spoke of it as a "fetus." I couldn't bring myself to call it a baby. Because, as far as I was concerned, it wasn't a baby. Regardless, I didn't want to lose "it." Not because I loved "it." But because my ego couldn't stand the idea of losing the fetus that far into the pregnancy. I was past my ten-week limit. By that time my sense of womanhood was on the line. Of course, I couldn't admit this to anyone.

Perhaps the decision isn't mine. Maybe it is you who should be asked whether or not you want to be born. You probably have seen as much of this world and human suffering as I have. You tell me. Do you want to be born? Will I be disturbing your world of peace and quiet by thrusting you into this not-so-quiet, not-so-peaceful world? Are there worse things than not being born?

Last night after completing one version of this chapter's conclusion, I tossed and turned and couldn't find a comfortable sleeping position. My fibroid was throbbing. And the baby was stirring around in me trying to find a comfortable position. Even now, as I type these last few lines, I can feel "her" tumbling inside me. She's been reading my journal. While rubbing my stomach with cream, my husband asked this morning whether I've been talking out loud to the baby, as the maternity books suggest. I tell him no. Talking out loud to "her" is for those who are not carrying her. She lives inside me, she hears every one of my thoughts. She knows she's wanted.

Hush. Mama's Gotta Go Bye-Bye.

I thought that I could exorcise myself of the demons of my childhood if I began by writing about my mother. That's what I thought. I thought I could write my way out of all the hurtful memories associated with growing up in an alcoholic home. That's what I thought. I thought I could write my way into intimate relationships. That's what I thought. One night I wrote until my knuckles were swollen. When I finished, I said to myself, "Surely now I am healed." That's what I said. But more than eight years have passed since I first wrote this chapter, and the demons have not vanished. We are just more cordial to one another.

I asked for intimacy. But in the relationship between mother and daughter, I found a frightened little girl instead.

My mother's mother, Lou Willie Clark, was short, round, and dark, with jet-black hair down her back. She had, I am told, an appetite for loving that embarrassed my grandfather. She was a Spartan woman who measured her pain with song. But like any "growing thing ripened too soon," to quote writer Jean Toomer, my grandmother eventually had to give up a part of herself before it was time. She gave up lust, though not her music, and lived to make a man out of my grandfather and a home for their seven children — four boys and three girls. One of those girls was my mother, Carrie Baker.

On Mother's Day in 1947, after Sunday morning church service, my grandmother was killed by a bullet intended for one of her sons. Shortly thereafter, my mother dropped out of school to help her elder sister care for their brothers and baby sister. About my mother's past, this is all I have been able to piece together.

Eight years ago my mother died an alcoholic. Eight years later, it still hurts to see these words spill across the page before me. It hurts to admit that my mother was an alcoholic, not that she is dead. She had been an alcoholic for as long as I can remember, certainly at least since I was a little girl. My most poignant memories of my childhood are of my older brother and me conspiring among ourselves for one of us to stall the bill collector at the door; or my father on the telephone, while the other tried — usually in vain — to wake Mama. After years of embarrassment and getting caught in lies, it was one of my mother's girlfriends — a drinking buddy and reputed licensed practical nurse — who showed me how, in emergencies, to wake my mother.

"Stick ice cubes on her chest," she demonstrated.

I can hear my mother crying and pleading with me, as I massaged her chest, to leave her alone. "Hush now," were my mother's words as I stroked her, "I'll be back in a little while."

It has been said before and deserves to be said again: When one person in the family has a drinking problem, the whole family has a drinking problem. One person contracts the disease, and everyone else dies from it. Children grow old before their time. They must learn to lie well to the outside world, to other members of the family, and to themselves. Parents fight with words and screams too bitter for children to be able to decide who is wrong and who has been wronged. Everyone must take sides, however. The whole nightmare is kept going by an endless succession of lies where the difference between what is real and what is not slowly pales.

When I am in physical pain, I think a lot about my mother. The unexplainable headache. The unusually tender breasts. The annoying pelvic exam. The sore pimple. I see her clearest when I stand in front of the mirror, which holds the jagged reflection of us both. Hers is the color of un-ground pepper; mine, the brown of old honey. No matter where I might go, she has made sure to remind me that I, too, am a woman from Sparta. There are those hips much too wide for the thin, slightly-bowed legs. Her big feet, one turned east and the other west, are mine, as are the long fingers that have never known the discipline of an instrument. But it is neither the hips nor the feet that make my mother's friends slap their knees when they see me and say in a declarative tone, "Lord, you must be Carrie's girl."

"Yes," I smile. It's the large oval eyes, I suppose, that confess that they've seen more than it's moral to tell, and the grin that is somewhere between shy and sly that make my mother's friends say that. The only difference between us, as I see it, is that I have my father's nose and, my mother used to add, my father's ways: stubborn and self-righteous. That, according to her, made me the girl who was "almost" her daughter. I am her eldest daughter. I look just like her but have never needed anything more than a cold Coke to quench my thirst.

In 1966 my mother gathered up her nerve and her drawers and walked out on my father and their five children. The little girl in me who felt powerless to save her always suspected that it was not my father, but me, the daughter who favored her, whom my mother was leaving. My father, whose testimony is not unimpeachable, says that it was after the birth of the first child that he first realized that my mother had a drinking problem. Nineteen years old, new to the big city of Atlanta, married to a gifted but poor, young colored man, stuck in the basement of his doting aunt's house, and burdened with the care of a newborn, my mother had more than enough to make her look for a melody in a bottle.

It is the fact that she was only nineteen that keeps me awake at night. At nineteen, I was in astronomy classes at an Ivy League women's college in New England, tracing the course of the galaxy and talking myself out of marrying a pre-med student from Long Island because his moon was in the wrong house. Nineteen years old. There must have been something more, I tell myself. "Believe me — being Black, female, poor, married with a new baby, and living with in-laws — that's enough to make you drink," says a girlfriend who ought to know. Actually, any two of the five is enough to make you stand on the corner and talk to yourself.

Less than a year after my mother left, my father remarried. Before he and Miss Nancy (that's what we called her, because she was our Sunday School teacher before she was our father's wife) could get back to my great-aunt's house to pick up the furniture he and my mother had shared, my mother had been there and gone. I can still see my father, brothers, and stepbrothers unloading the shredded green French Provincial sofa, along with the deeply slashed coffee and end tables. My sister and I turned our heads in horror. My father mumbled obscenities, and my stepmother bit her lip and muttered, "Lord, have mercy." Neither the assorted throw covers that were purchased over the years to drape the sofa nor the pints of finish used to stain those tables could hide, much less blot out, the fierceness of my mother's rage on the day she found out that my father would not come to get her. Because we could not afford to buy new furniture or have what was left professionally reupholstered, the sliced sofa and scratched tables served as permanent reminders of what my stepmother's happiness cost another woman. It was a long time before I could sit on the sofa again.

My mother loved us. I must believe that. She worked all day in a department-store bakery to buy us shoes and school tablets, came home to curse out the neighbors who wrongly accused her children of any impropriety (which in an apartment complex usually means stealing), and kept her house cleaner than most sober women. When money permitted, which was rare, or when she didn't give a damn about which bill collector had called that morning asking for "Willie" or "Carrie," she'd bring home a German-chocolate cake, her favorite, for dinner. The sight of her coming across the parking lot smiling slyly, her dark calloused hand swinging the white square box with the skinny string around it, sent us kids into a chorus of giggles, and we raced to see which one would get to her first to relieve her of such a delightful burden. Yes, my mother loved us. She bore us. She nursed us. She worked for us. She cried over us. She stayed up all night holding us when we were sick. Yes, my mother loved us. Even though she left us.

I know, without ever having been told, that her leaving us had nothing to do with her love for us. She exercised an option usually reserved for men. My mother loved her children *and* left them — for her own reasons. I just regret that she left before we could get to know each other. I had so many things to say to her — like how I was sorry for scratching the only record that made her smile: "Blowin' In The Wind" by Stevie Wonder.

It was the not-being-known that pained me the most when I was a little girl. Known the way I thought all my girlfriends' mothers knew them: "This is Patricia. She is moody and reflective and needs more attention than my other children." I could live with my mother's drinking. And I did. I could live with the haunting sounds of her and my father's battles (they fought unapologetically before us all) that drove me into the bathroom to play church and pull out my hair. I can now forgive her for teaching me how to lie with a straight face to my father, to neighbors, to creditors, and to my playmates. (It was a lesson that took years to unlearn.) I could live with these horrible memories and more. And I have. But it was the not-being-known for who I singularly was that sent me into the arms of women teachers, neighbors, friends' mothers, and perfect strangers — women who did not have the onus of providing for me and, so, had the luxury of listening and talking to me.

What my mother was not able to give me, I learned to steal emotionally from other women. I longed for my own private smile from my mother. When it did not come, I learned to be smart enough to be refreshing and witty enough to be charming for others. Being the top student in my class was my way of securing the teacher's attention and affection. I fought anyone who tried to take that away from me. To those beautiful colored teachers from Albany State, Alabama State, and Fort Valley State who took the time to re-braid a loose plait and spread Jergens lotion across my ashy face, my answers were bright instead of sassy and my opinions thoughtful instead of womanish. They loved me enough to beat me, but not for the same reason as my mother.

They beat me into believing that there was no limit to who I could become. My mother beat me because she was afraid of what I *might* become. At night, lying scared and restless in my bed, I dreamed of those sweet-smelling colored women from state colleges. I also dreamed of a woman in a distant room, listening to sad, sad music and the bottomless sound of liquid splashing into a glass. I longed for that woman, singing her sad song, to come tuck me in and reassure me that the shadow across the ceiling was not Billy Goat Gruff who'd come to terrorize me for my sins. I tried to imagine her coming into the room with a broom in one hand and rocking me until I was exhausted with love with the other hand.

Next in significance to those lovely colored teachers, Miss Susie Skinner and Mrs. Daisy Henderson, and the women in the neighborhood who sent me to the store for Kotex, were my paper dolls. Those pale, thin white girls in pretty lace underwear and contrived smiles depended on me to speak for them, dress them, fight for them, love them, and give their cardboard lives meaning. In exchange for giving them life, they taught me two things: how to love and how to heal myself. When their heads fell off, which was often, there were always the ladies in the Sears and Roebuck catalogs. Then there were the dolls made from Coke bottles. The coarse rope that tied store-bought collard greens became their hair.

I now remember how much delight my mother took in buying these things for me. Perhaps she knew. (My God, did she know?) Her buying me paper dolls and ordering catalogs from which she never made purchases and spending money she didn't have on Sally, the pink plastic doll with omniscient eyes who came to my shoulder and danced with me — was this my mother's way of creating a world she was unable to give me? Is this why she never laughed when I'd spend the entire day in the closet with my dolls and, later, turned her head when I grew to be a woman and still had long eloquent conversations with myself? In her liquor bottle she found what she must have hoped I would find in my dolls.

Even with all those educated colored teachers whom I knew and loved, it was my mother, the skinny, bowlegged girl from Sparta with a ninth-grade education, who was the first feminist I ever knew. Everywhere we moved until I was twelve (which was, at last count, thirteen times), no matter how short our tenure, my mother always surrounded herself with women. They drank together, played cards together, danced together, laughed together, fished together, fought one another, scratched one another's heads, and always protected one another from the wrath of husbands, lovers, and boyfriends. For sure, she loved men — my brothers, her brothers, Jackie Wilson, Solomon Burke, and sometimes my father. But she *needed* women. "She is my girlfriend," she'd blurt out in defense whenever my father accused her of hanging out with "them women" more than he thought she should.

When they were not drinking, my mother and her girlfriends busied themselves with the ceremonies of womanhood: shucking corn, snapping beans, shelling peas, kneading dough, mending hems, folding clothes, and fanning themselves with the hems of their dresses. Invariably, a little girl, like my sister or myself, could be found kneeling between some woman's legs getting her hair combed. "Girl, hush." "Child, please." "Heifer, no." One woman would yell across the room to another over the noises of children and a scratched record. Their words sashayed over our heads — dancing, curtsying, bowing, and finally embracing one another in holy communion. Love of women and appreciation for the sound of a woman saying, "Go on, girl, with you' bad self" — these were my mother's exquisite gifts to my sister and me.

Over the years I have tried to forget my mother. There are many Black women who have not been able or eager to talk about our less-than-perfect, our outrageous, mothers. It would be like playing the dozens on ourselves.

It would be counterrevolutionary, in fact. We have simply sat and nodded while others talked about the magnificent women who bore and raised them and who, along with God, made a way out of no way. We recited their poems. We bought their novels. We paid to hear them lecture about the invincible strength and genius of the Black mother, knowing full well that the image could be as bogus as the one of the happy slave. But we smiled, clapped, and shouted, too, because we knew that what our mothers were forced to become was not what they had dreamed for themselves; we knew that part of the healing is learning how to rejoice over other folks' blessings; and we knew that our mothers would have wanted us to know that there was another way.

The easiest thing in the world would be to romanticize my mother's drinking, see it as the muted need of a repressed artist who sought to drink in the fullness of life. That would make a great sermon or poem and would certainly help me get some sleep at night. The next easiest thing would be to blame my father for my mother's illness. This I have done. But the truth is never that simple. Besides, both scenarios have a way of overlooking the very real fact that there was an element of choice. Notwithstanding culture and circumstance, my mother chose to drink and retreat, rather than remain sober and fight. No, she did not intend to become an alcoholic. I know that now. She just wanted to get through another day. She did not intend to leave her five children. She just had to get out of that house. My stepmother would always say, "Neetie, I love being a mother. I just get tired, however, of mothering. Sometimes I want to walk out that door and never look back." But she didn't. My mother did. I've had enough experience with depression and madness to know that, no matter how absolute the loneliness or the madness, there is always that one final moment – however fleeting – when one can still choose not to let go.

I cannot forget my mother. Though not as sturdy as others, she was my bridge. When I needed to get across, she steadied herself long enough for me to run across safely. For that, I am grateful. She left before she could crumble before my eyes. Sometimes, when I visited her, I would catch myself studying her out of the corner of my eye, wondering what really drove her to drink. The poet in me searched frantically for the subtle turn in the drama. But the woman in me told me that if what I knew was enough to keep me awake, then I could not begrudge my mother the desire to sleep through it all.

My mother died alone in Atlanta. Her life was filled with her grandchildren, soap operas, her girlfriends, a man friend, and fishing. Our lives took radically different courses. I am fulfilled by my ministry and my writing. She was plagued by the kind of health problems that come with drinking. When I am depressed, I pray and write poems. When she was depressed, she drank and waited for a disability check that never came. When I am happy, I strut and write sermons. When she was happy, she fished, made centerpieces of pine cones and needles – and took a little nip. I tried giving my mother my God. And being the well-bred southern lady that she was, she never refused a gift given from the heart. She would simply smile, nod her head, and put the God I offered in the shoe box she kept on the shelf of her closet where she stored her insurance policy and scraps of material for a future quilt.

My professional ministry is mainly to women. I preach to them. I cry, shout, pray, and laugh with them. I encourage them to believe that their lives and their situations can be changed. But many times, when I was in the presence of my own mother, I could not think of a word to say. Songs, poems and sermons escaped me. "I am a feminist and a minister," I would say to myself, "but I cannot reach my mother." Yet she never held that against me.

My mother died in December more than eight years ago. Perhaps this time when I go home for the holidays, I will visit her grave site on a hill not far from where my younger brother, her youngest son, is buried. (I have never visited my mother's grave site before.) Perhaps when I visit her, I will tell her about that Stevie Wonder record. Perhaps I will stand over my mother's grave and call to her the way her girlfriends would call to her when they visited the house: "Yoo-hoo, girl." And I will see her coming to the screen door of my imagination with an expression of mock irritation on her face. And I will hear the sharp ring of the voice that sounds much like my own when she says, "Girl, hush."

Daddy's Girl

It's often easier for a woman to write about her relationship with her mother than it is to write about her relationship with her father. While there are lots of occasions for and incentives to do the former, there is hardly any precedent for the latter. A mother's role in her daughter's life is viewed in this society as essential and conspicuous. But a father's role in his daughter's life remains ambiguous and relatively unexplored.

For years I resisted writing about my relationship with my father. Marriage, however, prompted me to think about it. Many instances arose in the early days of my marriage when I knew that I was responding to something more ancient and insidious than my husband's behavior or attitude. Like most daughters in their relationships with their fathers, from my observations of my father's behavior in our home, I extrapolated a whole set of assumptions about the roles of men (and women). My father was someone to be feared, not loved. (And, for years, he seemed content with his children's fear.)

In short, I grew up believing that men were creatures to be loved fearfully. Strange how neither my religion, my God, the Scriptures — nor even my husband's love, thus far — have been able to revoke my father's example.

I asked for intimacy. But I found my father's face in my mirror instead.

———————————————

—————————

I have this habit. I tend to buy every book I come across on father-daughter relationships, but I never read them. I bring them home and dump them on my desk, never to open them. I can't bring myself to read even the first page. It's as though something in me doesn't want to peer into that chapter of my life. Of all the topics on the modern woman that I can pontificate about *ad nauseam*, says my husband, the topic of daughters and their fathers is the only one that makes me utterly incoherent. I know it's because my relationship with my own father is tormentingly ambivalent. My relationship with him is the one aspect of my life where prayer does not avail and where my faith becomes absurd. How do you forgive someone who has not changed?

Have you ever noticed how few father-daughter stories there are in the Bible? I have. Of course, there are even fewer mother-daughter stories; but that's a matter for another chapter. The greatest preponderance of parent-child stories is about mothers and their sons. Of the three father-daughter stories that come to mind, two are insufferable and one is touching.

The first one is about the Genesis character Lot, nephew of Abraham, and his two daughters. Fearing that with the destruction of Sodom and Gomorrah they would die barren, Lot's daughters conspired between themselves to trick their father into having sex with them — or so the narrator would have us believe. The story was evidently first told as an aetiological tale to explain the origin of two of Israel's neighbors to the east, the Moabites and the Ammonites (the two sons born to the daughters were named Moab and Ben-Ammi, respectively). Misbegotten kinsmen would be the kindest way to explain them, born out of the impulsive, sinful, desperate initiative of two women — or so the narrator would have us believe. Lot, who elsewhere in Genesis comes across at best as a shady sort of fellow, is painted as innocent and helpless before the wiles of his daughters.[1] This is not the kind of story that helps to heal the wounds of incest.

The second father-daughter story that comes to mind is found in the book of Judges. It is the story of Jephthah and his daughter.[2] Here, a father murdered his daughter in order to honor a rash, foolish vow he made to God. The daughter dutifully, pitifully, submitted to her father's obsession with honor. This story about scapegoating, betrayal of trust, senseless submission, and child sacrifice is almost too unbearable to read. Of course, I wouldn't want to have to choose between it and the story of Lot and his two daughters.

In all the healing accounts in the gospels, there is only one in which a father entreated Jesus on behalf of his daughter. His name was Jairus, and he was a ruler of the synagogue. I wonder if it's significant that the sick child was his only daughter.[3] So desperate was Jairus for his daughter to be healed that he, a synagogue official, fell at the carpenter's feet. Either he loved his daughter or he was aware of how undeserving he was to petition the Savior.

I think of this story and wonder whether my own father prayed for me when I was rushed to the hospital at age eight for appendicitis. I was desperately sick. I wonder . . . he has never been, to my knowledge, a praying man. Even when my younger brother was struck by a taxi and left for months in a cast from the waist down, I don't remember seeing my father pray. I'm sure he was frightened, anxious, and concerned; he just couldn't bring himself to pray.

[1] Genesis 13:8-2; 19:8
[2] See my chapter "A Crying Shame" in *Just A Sister Away: A Womanist Vision of Women's Relationships in the Bible.* San Diego: LuraMedia, 1988.
[3] Luke 8:42

When I was a little girl, I looked up to my father. And until recently, whatever notions I've had about what makes a man masculine, I have gleaned from watching him. To be a man was, in my mind, to be dark and strong like my father. He was my confidant. He was my protector. He was my hero. When he was in a good mood, he'd swing me in the air, rub his stubby beard against my face, and laugh as I squirmed with delight. My father would get out of his bed when I screamed at nights and search my closet and look underneath my bed for shadows and strange sounds that I swore lurked about. And for that, I forgave him of his moody, hot-tempered, and terribly violent ways, which often left him sullen and distant from the family. And because he raised us after our mother left, I pretended not to notice one spring afternoon that my father never cried as the family stood over the casket of his youngest son.

My father's volcanic moods, strong dark arms, and stoic ways have always embodied the essence of masculinity for me. The men I've loved and fought the fiercest were, in many instances, men just like my father. But when I married, I married a man who is, in many ways, the complete opposite of my father.

My husband is gentle, nurturing, soft-spoken, open, and articulate about his feelings; he weeps when he recalls painful childhood memories and prefers not to be aroused from his sleep. Where my father frightened me (and the rest of his children) into obedience, my husband loves me into submission. My father's masculinity is what I remember, but my husband's masculinity is what I need.

Still, marriage teaches me every day that, despite all my savvy, I haven't quite rid myself of my father's model of masculinity. After all, my father not only impressed upon me what it meant to be masculine, he also taught me what it meant for me to be feminine. And little girls who want to please their fathers make the best students for lessons on what is expected of women. So I learned what it meant to be feminine by trial and error. If my father was sullen, uncommunicative, hostile, and dogmatic, I learned to charm him by being chatty, devoted, receptive, and compliant. If he was warm, jovial, talkative, and patient, I engaged him by being chatty, devoted, receptive, and compliant. I learned my role well.

But is femininity really something little girls learn? Or is femininity (and masculinity, for that matter) a set of behavior patterns that is as innate to our genders as our biological differences? "Feminine" is traditionally defined as nurturing, understanding, supportive, intuitive, emotional, passive, sentimental, indecisive, and impulsive. "Masculine," on the other hand, is commonly thought to be aggressive, analytical, detached, independent, ambitious, and strong. To the extent that these traits actually reflect male and female behavior patterns – and there is considerable debate as to whether they do – the question remains: Is it indeed the "nature" of women to be compassionate and emotional, and men to be macho and daring? Or are we socialized by our culture into certain patterns of behavior, ways of behaving that get rewarded when exemplified in the appropriate sex and punished or ridiculed when exhibited by the other?

Of course, mothers have their own opinions about how masculine and feminine traits develop.

"It's in the water!" exclaims a friend, mother of two and an algebra teacher. "How else did I end up with this chauvinist for a son and lady-in-waiting for a daughter?" Azura insists that, despite her best efforts, her children have grown up to be people she doesn't know.

"Here I am raising my son and daughter in a nonsexist environment where their father and I share equally in the housework and in their rearing, mindful to use inclusive language (like 'humankind' instead of 'mankind' and 'God the creator' rather than 'God the Father'), giving them toys both sexes can play with – and what do you know?" Azura falls back in her seat. "My son comes in here from college, sits at my table, and argues that women should not be ministers. My daughter is at the other end of the table chattering away with her father about this cute med student she's met and how grand it would be to be a doctor's wife."

Behavior scientists differ in their accounting for the differences between women and men. The Swiss psychologist Carl Jung, for example, writing during the first half of the century, argued that every person is born with qualities of the opposite sex within them, not simply in the biological sense, but also in the psychological sense of attitudes and feelings. The feminine side of the male psyche, which Jung referred to as *anima*, and the masculine side of the female psyche, the *animus*, are significant to the survival of each sex because they facilitate appropriate responses to and understanding of the opposite sex. If the personality is to be well-adjusted and harmoniously balanced, argued Jung, a man must be able to express his feminine traits and a woman, her masculine traits.

"What happens in our society is that one side of our personality is repressed to the detriment of both sides," argues a psychology professor friend of mine. "When little girls are aggressive or strong-willed, they are branded as 'tom boyish' and are eventually forced to suppress the *animus* within. Boys who won't fight back or who like taking dance lessons, if they want to be accepted by their male peers, will eventually learn to loathe the *anima* within.

"Both sexes," he adds, "must give up very important sides of themselves to be accepted, and in so doing neither ever really fulfills his or her potential, not just as male or female, but as human beings."

Jungian psychology may insist that each sex is born with both masculine and feminine traits and, as such, is born capable of empathy and understanding for the other, but when we look around, it's clear that the theory isn't very often lived out in reality. The fact is, there are sharp differences between women and men, differences that cause them to lock horns over not only fleeting gains, like money and power, but also over matters of love and intimacy. They find themselves in battles where they can't seem to understand each other; in modern jargon it's called "the battle of the sexes."

The malaise began, according to some, with the social upheaval of the sixties when the roles and the rules governing the sexes changed. Before then, as the saying goes, "Men were men and girls were girls." Now, with women seeking parity with men in the public sector, men suing for alimony from their ex-wives, and both sexes seeking restitution for loveless unions, the definitions of feminine and masculine behavior have become blurred. But the truth is that, while the rules may have changed, the roles all too often remain firmly in place. For example, today men may be willing to concede that women are as rational as they, and women may claim they welcome men who are unashamed of crying. But when it comes to who is responsible for raising the kids and who should make the most money in the family, things tend to remain much the same. Traits may be interchangeable, but roles are not.

My investment banker friend Phyllis admits that the major reason she avoids any discussion about marriage with Michael, a high school teacher with whom she's lived for the last three years, is because she can't bring herself to marry a man who makes less money than she does. "It's bizarre, I'll admit," she says, "but I have this Byzantine notion that the woman's salary should 'help out' and not be the backbone of the household." Asked whether she's talked with Michael about how she feels, she replies, "I can't tell him how I feel. He'll only withdraw into his shell and shut me out for days. He reminds me of my father. I guess that's why I love him and stay with him."

As I've already noted, a very real part of being my father's daughter was learning to read my father's moods. The whole emotional well-being of the family from day to day depended on somebody's ability to read Daddy's face, mood, and movements. Because I was his favorite, the job usually fell to me. And I've been reading men's faces, moods, and movements ever since. And I must say, I've misjudged a few in my life and have pigeon-holed even more.

The problem comes when I start interpreting every frown on a man's face as anger, when he may just be concentrating; his quietness as a lack of savvy, when he could be just shy. Our preconceived notions of how a "real man" or "real woman" behaves make us try to put people into boxes that are of our own making. And when they don't fit the boxes we've so adroitly designed for them, we prefer to penalize them – or more often, ourselves – rather than change our thinking.

Imagine, for example, in a battle of words, you are the better of the two, and yet you insist that his masculine duty is to negotiate with sales agents and haggle with repair people – even though he hates it. You interpret his failure to do so as a lack of caring on his part.

Or, you're afraid to go into the manager's office and ask him for a shot at the supervisory job that just opened up in one of his other divisions? You don't want to seem too pushy or aggressive. Meanwhile, you keep on typing for and serving coffee to your ambitious supervisor.

Or, you refuse to go out with the guy at your church because he's two inches shorter than you, and you prefer to date someone who is at least three inches taller – even though no one taller has asked you out lately. It's hard, you say, to feel feminine with a man you've got to look down to see. You have your image to think of.

Stereotypes cheat us of possibilities. And they are sure to keep us from getting to know people for who they really are: individuals with their own distinctive personalities and styles. For, in reality, human beings are far more complex and enigmatic than our tidy categories and near-sighted norms can account for.

Still, old habits are hard to break. While writing this article, I leave my computer three times to go downstairs and check if my husband needs me. His quietness, which I mistake for sullenness, makes me think something is wrong. And if there is, it is my feminine duty to fix it. The third time, I find him rummaging through the refrigerator, crumbs falling from his beard.

"Are you all right?" I ask.

"Renita, I know how to feed myself." He looks sternly up from his search.

Like my father, my husband doesn't mince words. I turn on my heels and climb the stairs back to my study. I remind myself that my rescuing days are over. I don't have to fear that if I don't anticipate his needs, interpret his moods, and pacify his whims, then I've failed as "Daddy's girl." But my father is my only father, and his is the only example I have. And sometimes it is easier for me to settle for old patterns of behavior than it is to invent myself.

A Love that Lets Go

Whether it is the sight of a Somalian mother holding her child's emaciated frame close to her sagging breast; or a mother staring dazedly into the camera as she recounts the death of her son on the streets of Los Angeles; or a mother standing stoically over a patch of the AIDS quilt with her son's name on it — the image of each ought to burn in our memories. Women have had to bury their children for centuries. And they have had to stand by and watch their sons die far too often.

The relationship between a mother and her son is an intimate one. It is as sublime as it is complex. It is ancient and it is familiar. It begs for words though it defies description. We turn to the untold story of Mary and her son Jesus as a way of acknowledging that there are some relationships that not even death can rob us of.

She asked for intimacy. But in a mother's relationship with her son, she learns that there are some experiences of intimacy that words do not illumine; they only disappoint.

———————————————

———————————

My son was dying, and there was nothing I could do to help or save him. When I heard the child whom I had dutifully raised to fear and revere God cry out in pain, asking why God had forsaken him, I wanted to scream. I had asked that question of God a thousand times already.

My son had tried to prepare me for this day. But what mother is ever prepared to witness her child's death? No mother wants to live that long. I certainly didn't. Even though he had warned me many times that he would die at the hands of men, I secretly prayed that, for once, he would be mistaken. But he was not. Even though there was a side of me that understood that it had to be this way — that this was the purpose for which he'd come into the world, that he had to die in order to live again, that this was the will of the Creator — still I resented him, and the Creator, for torturing me this way. Why did my son have to die this way? I didn't care about all the lives he was saving by dying. I didn't want him to die. I wanted him to come down and prove that he was not a fraud, not deranged, not a religious fanatic, not a blasphemer. I wanted him to do something, anything, but die like a common criminal. As his mother, I wanted to urge him to do something. But I kept silent. I'd known for some time that this day was coming.

Among the women huddling a few feet away from him were my sister, who wept with her eyes closed, refusing to look at his feeble pose; Salome, who muttered and prayed unintelligibly as she dabbed her eyes with the hem of her veil; Mary of Magdala, who knelt on the ground sobbing, her eyes transfixed on the nails in his feet; and the others, who variously cried and collapsed. I, however, stood quietly by, neither weeping nor wailing. Mine were dry tears. The man hanging on the cross in the hot afternoon sun was not my nephew, not just the Messiah, not simply a friend; he was my son, my first born. And I stood there at the foot of his cross powerless, aghast, staring up at my child.

His features were almost indistinguishable for the blood issuing from his temples, the expression of agony on his face, and the scourge marks across his body. I couldn't see his eyes for the blood.

The only time I felt my body go limp was when I heard the executioner's hammer. Resting his knee on the inside of my son's forearm, I watched him probe my son's wrist to find the hollow spot. When he raised his hammer over the nail head and brought it down with force, I could hear the wails of women throughout the crowd. But none of them could match my son's outcry.

Nor the one in my head. Some of those whom I recognized as his followers turned their heads. Some buried their faces. Others walked away. I clutched my collar with one hand and beat my chest with the other. A jolt of pain tore through me. Right then the words of a just man in Jerusalem, from years ago when Joseph and I had presented our son for circumcision, came to my mind: *". . . and a sword will pierce your own soul, too."*

I looked up in time to see the soldiers lifting the crossbeam with my son's writhing body onto the upright beam. The tormented expression on his face shredded my insides. When the beams were secured, the next part of the ritual was begun: nailing the feet in place. It had to be done just so. His feet had to be pushed upward on the cross to prevent the kind of rapid draining of the blood that would occur had his feet been nailed straight. One of his disciples tried to bury my face in his chest to protect me. But I pushed his hand gently away. I could not cry, but I promised myself that I would look. I didn't cry so I could see my son dying. Death I understand. God knows, I've buried my share of family and friends. It is the act and agony of dying that I find the hardest to witness. Especially when the one dying is your child. Having to watch the accelerated decay of your child's body before your very eyes is torment. Your eyes fix on portions of his decaying body that you remember were once soft folds of baby flesh. Before you now is a body that is frail and contorted, too fragile to caress. But you remember when the feel of him at your breast made you pull him close, not wanting to let go. Dying, as far as I am concerned, is death's cruel sense of humor.

His swollen face rested on his left shoulder. This meant that the thorns the soldiers had just placed on his head had pierced both his temples and his shoulder. His arms were stretched above his head in the shape of a V.

Blood and sweat streamed down his body. A large blob of both gathered in the thick coarse beard I'd always admired. His breathing was weak, his chest barely heaved. From the waist down, he appeared lifeless. His feet were unrecognizable; the swelling had begun to swallow the five-inch nail. His body looked like a withering, gnarled vine against the backdrop of the cypress beam that held his body.

Even though I had tried to prepare myself for this day, still, when the time came I was not ready.

The sight of his barely clad frame dragging through the streets the thirty-pound crossbeam across his bloody, lacerated right shoulder had been difficult to witness. I wanted to cover his body with my own. All around me, and the disciple who stood by me, crowds pressed about, shaking their heads, gawking, jeering, asking questions. Children asked their parents what death was. Adults asked each other what the three had done to deserve death. And pilgrims who were en route to Jerusalem to observe the Sabbath looked away in disgust, not wanting to see Romans put Jews to death. When the procession reached Golgotha, where three upright cypress beams stood for just such occasions, a hush fell over everyone. The hill smelled of death. I clasped the disciple's hand.

Over the last several months, I had found out everything I

could about the Roman custom of execution. I had thought I could prepare myself.

It was an efficient form of execution, and the Romans had the procedure down to a science. Although the Phoenicians had been the first to introduce crucifixion as a form of capital punishment – after having tried execution by spear, boiling in oil, impalement, stoning, strangulation, drowning, and burning – it was the Romans who perfected the procedure. The Phoenicians had found that death by crucifixion was too sudden to be a deterrent. It took Roman imagination to devise a means by which to prolong death, something long enough to torture the prisoner, but short enough to hold the attention of the average onlooker: three hours would do it. It began with a scourging, which was aimed at exhausting the prisoner to hurry along his expiration. Then there was the march through the city with the crossbeam tied upon his shoulders, also aimed at exhaustion and humiliation. And then there came the crucifixion itself. Sometimes wine was given as an act of mercy in order to dull the prisoner's senses to the pain. Hearing the way the Roman soldiers roared with laughter after offering my son something in a jar, I knew it had not been wine, but probably vinegar.

But there is no way for a mother to prepare for her child's death. Not for his death, and certainly not for his dying. You can't prepare. You can only witness and watch a part of you die with him.

Out of the corner of my eye I saw my husband, Joseph, standing off a distance with a pained expression on his face. He had refused to come with me when word came that our son had been taken before the Tribunal. He feigned being busy in his shop. There had always been a gentle awkwardness between the two. But from where I stood, I could tell that the sight of the mutilated body Joseph had once bathed in cold towels was more than he, too, could bear. He did not look in my direction. I always felt that somehow he blamed me for the fact that this child who, though well-mannered and respectful, never quite regarded him as a father. Before he turned and walked away, Joseph too wept.

While everyone else wept, I looked on and remembered.

When my son was a newborn in my arms, he would look up at me with trusting, innocent, eager eyes, eyes that seemed always to be asking questions of me for which I had no answers. My only way of answering him was to hold him tightly in my arms and pray that I would always be able to protect him. I wanted to hold him and never let him go. Even then, I knew that one day he would break my heart.

In truth, life with him was always life without him. He never really belonged to me. Even his conception was shrouded in mystery. My pregnancy had created quite a stir in the village where I lived. Some said I had been raped. Some said I'd been immoral. Some called me an outright liar when I spoke to them about angels, visions, and voices. There were times when I myself didn't know what to believe. It had all happened so quickly. I felt like I was anything but a woman who was blessed among women. I didn't want to bear the Christ; I wanted to have a son. It almost cost me Joseph. Although my husband eventually believed me, I felt he never quite forgave me. The truth is, while Jesus was my son, he was never quite my child. He never really belonged to me.

But when he was born, I understood why mothers die for their sons. A son is a mother's obsession in a way a daughter rarely is. For his is the first male love that is lavished upon her without her asking.

She neither has to compete for it or earn it. Her father's love and attention are always complicated by her mother's presence; her brother's love is always compromised by her mother and siblings; and her husband's love is rarely unconditional. For a time, her son's love is the only male love for which she doesn't have to compete, doesn't have to seduce, doesn't have to earn. An infant son touches his mother, but does not coerce her.

He loves her, but cannot possess her. For the first time in her life, she controls the way she is loved by a male. For the first time, she can fashion the way she wants to be loved. He is a part of her, but he is not like her — which makes his every impulse bewitching. His maleness fascinates her. His difference arouses her. He is her son, and he is a stranger, and he loves her. The combination is arresting. And no matter how old he becomes, no matter where he goes, she can always be satisfied to know that she, his mother, was his first love.

There were times when I resented the life my son had chosen.

He was never home for the holidays, and he never remembered my birthday. His ministry was first. In fact, it was the only thing in his life. He gave me no grandchildren. He slept wherever he could lay his head, I am told, even though he didn't have to; he ate whatever he could, even though he didn't have to. He could always come home, but he never chose to. I accepted that, sort of. He was never mine. And he was always just a trot away from peril. He lived under constant threat to his life. But so did we, his family. It started as far back as the time when he was born. Even then, Joseph and I had to flee to Egypt to save his life. But the threat of death never seemed to faze him. Why didn't he ever think about his family: the toil that his lifestyle took on us? the ridicule, the stares, the interrogations, the rumors, the threats? the ostracism?

It seemed that everywhere my son went, he made more enemies than converts. Even our neighbors in Nazareth doubted his ministry. They took no pride in their native son. Even after his first sermon taken from the scroll of Isaiah, I overheard the old men asking one another, "Wasn't that Joseph's son?" They could not understand how, nor were they willing to believe, that a carpenter's son could be so learned in matters of the law and the prophets as he had proven to be. The fact that he spoke with such authority seemed only to irritate them. My son left home that day and never returned to Nazareth, to his family, to his home — not really.

It was ironic that the one who went about bringing healing and hope to other families would remain, for the most part, estranged from his own. Imagine the insult when, on one of the few occasions I, along with his sisters and brothers, tried to see him, he sent word back asking who his mother was. I was shocked and hurt. Who did he think he was? Busy or not, ordained or not, that was no way to talk to his mother! I bit my tongue, regained my poise, and walked away.

After all I'd done for him! I'd washed his butt when he didn't know he had one; I'd sucked the phlegm from his nostrils when he couldn't breathe; I'd stayed up all night when he had been sick with fever; I'd taught him to read; I'd prayed for him when he couldn't pray for himself; I had been the one who encouraged him to perform his first miracle by turning the jars of water into wine. Not that he owed me anything. But he could have shown me some respect. Had he gotten too big to come see about his own people?

The soldier's laughter brought me back me to the cross. Some were kneeling at his feet gambling. Others were taunting him. Someone had placed a sign over his head that read, *"The King of the Jews."*

When the rumor had begun that he was speaking of himself as the Messiah, I knew that it was the beginning of the end. My people have no tolerance for those with Messianic complexes. Religious charlatans, fakes, quacks, and fanatics they may countenance, for a while. But Messiahs are invariably put to death. To the Jew, the search for the Messiah is a national pastime. It is as though we prefer the speculation to the real thing. Centuries of Jewish thinking have been devoted to the predictions, and no good Jew tires of hearing of them: The sages all agreed that the Messiah would be of the House of David; the prophets warned that his birth would be unknown to many; the scholars maintained that after he came, the only holy day would be the Day of Atonement; and everyone agreed that all those from the ten tribes of Israel who were scattered would be brought back from the corners of the world to once again live in their own land — on the condition, of course, that they repented for their sins. The only problem was that no one knew what the Messiah would look like. Would he come as a King, a priest, a prophet, a rabbi? Of course, no one imagined him to be a carpenter's son turned fisherman. Whether or not he had already come was the preoccupation of the sages. Whether or not these were days of his coming was the preoccupation of the commoner. Whether or not my son was the Messiah had already been decided.

Finally, my son lifted his head and looked in my direction. I moved closer. I wanted him to see that I was there; powerless, lost, tormented, and empty, but there. His voice was faint. The only word I could make out was "woman." I thought I would buckle under the sound of his voice. Tears welled in my eyes, but I fought them back. I wanted to see my son. I felt my head whirling. Didn't he recognize me?

"... *woman ... woman ... woman ...*"

His words tore at my heart. Why couldn't he call me "mother"? Why, even in death, was he keeping his distance? I could feel the disciple's arm tighten around me. It was as though my son were giving me away to a stranger. I was his *mother*. Didn't I mean anything to him? Didn't he remember? Why didn't he call me "mother"? I needed him to call me mother once more before it was over. Say it, say it, I screamed in my head. I needed to hear him call out to me.

Thinking back on it, perhaps, just perhaps, had he allowed himself to think of me as his mother, he might have come down from that cross. Perhaps he knew that, in the end, I needed a Savior more than I needed a son.

In the distance I heard the crack of thunder as his body sagged one last time into the shape of a V. I knew then that it was time to let my beloved son go. And so I did. But first I cried.

The Leah Syndrome

I am told that I am better at describing unhappiness than I am happiness. And there may be some truth to this. I don't quite know why this is so, though I have my suspicions. I've always found the blemished side of human behavior infinitely more fascinating. And try though I may to be otherwise, I am always drawn to stories about death, disappointment, betrayal, heartache, and addictive behavior. I seem to have far more empathy for tragedy than interest in good fortune.

But my fascination with suffering doesn't make me morbid, necessarily. It just makes me the kind of person who is always searching for the sublime in sorrow. Sometimes I find it. Sometimes I don't. But one thing is for sure: Everything I've ever learned well, I've learned from pain. And no pain is more poignant and deafening than the pain that comes in relationships — especially relationships between men and women. I find myself always coming back to peer at this pain.

And when my own experiences of painful relationships are too grotesque to recount, or those of my friends too confidential to disclose, I take recourse in the stories of women and men in the Bible. Some of us learn better by seeing our reflection in ancient stories.

All that I ask from these stories about the relationships between men and women is something I can recognize — something passionate, something memorable, something urgent, something intimate.

The only thing worse than loving a man who doesn't love you is loving a man who loves someone else. Perhaps the second thing worse than loving a man who doesn't love you is loving a man who loves your sister. And the only thing worse than all of the above is having sex with a man who hates you. Of course, he doesn't hate you enough to leave you — after all, what man can resist a compliant woman. Rather, he hates you enough to make sure you remain dependent upon him.

And, unfortunately, you don't love yourself or hate the situation enough to leave him.

This is called the Leah Syndrome.

The Leah Syndrome refers to women who love too much, women who conspire against themselves in relationships, women who refuse to let go, women who use their sexuality to snare men they're better off without, women who allow what the men in their lives think of them to become what they think of themselves, women who get involved in relationships that are a re-creation of painful memories from their childhood.

It is called the Leah Syndrome.

Leah's story is found in the book of Genesis. Of course, the twenty-ninth chapter of Genesis is not Leah's story at all, but Jacob's story — or more precisely, Israel's story. But for now I will call it Leah's story because it is the least that we can do for Leah since she didn't do anything for herself for quite awhile.

Calling it Leah's story, of course, is also to shift the attention away from Jacob and what Jacob did to Leah. After all, Jacob had the right to love whomever he wished. Calling it Leah's story is also to refrain from casting too much light on Rachel, or what Rachel did to Leah. After all, Rachel had a right to be loved. Calling it Leah's story means that we have to focus on what Leah did to Leah.

Leah was Jacob's second choice. Having contracted with Laban to serve him for seven years for the hand of his younger daughter, Rachel, Jacob was tricked by Laban and given Leah instead. So great was his love for Rachel, however, that Jacob hired himself out to Laban for another seven years to get the woman of his choice. Meanwhile, Leah was like a second beer: The first one quenches your thirst, the second one quenches your greed. You drink it because it's there.

This story is about the lengths to which Leah went in order to get her husband to love her. From what we can tell, she failed in her mission. She could have by the story's end, however, succeeded in attracting the affections of the intractable swindler she married. We're not sure how much better off she'd been had she succeeded. Worse yet, Leah could have persisted on in her pathetic obsession to make Jacob love her. But – fortunately, for Leah – eventually she came to herself.

Meanwhile, however, it's a familiar story: Jacob punished Leah for not being Rachel by touching Leah and thinking of Rachel. Leah punished herself for not being Rachel by doing everything imaginable to make Jacob love her.

It is called the Leah Syndrome.

Nowhere does it mention that Leah loved Jacob. We assume that she did. Nonetheless, you might ask, how do we explain her desperate behavior? When did love and desperation become the same? When does it cease to be love and become fear instead? The fear of being alone. The fear of being unloved. The fear of being unlovable. The fear of being anything but uppermost on his mind, as he is on yours.

Now, whether Leah loved Jacob, we can only guess. One thing is sure, however: Leah was addicted to a relationship with Jacob. Relationship addicts do not have husbands or lovers; they have hostages. Their self-esteem is tied to their relationship. Relationship addicts never let go of past relationships, and when the present one is on the rocks, another one is always in the making. Relationship addicts are obsessed about their lack of a relationship, and they will do anything to stay in a relationship, be in a relationship, find a relationship. A pseudo-relationship is better than no relationship. The fantasy is to be coupled with somebody, anybody. They may want to get married — even though they have no one in mind. Even though they have never been married and don't have the faintest idea what marriage is really like. Even though they don't know one married couple who is happily married. Even though every relationship they've ever been involved in has been an abysmal failure. They just want to get married. They are addicted to being in a relationship, any relationship.[1]

Let's get personal. When you are addicted to relationships, you will go to any lengths to be in a relationship, even if it is only on the fringe of one. Which is why you have settled for a married man. Which is why your girlfriend whom you invited to church joined the prison outreach ministry and wound up becoming engaged to a prisoner who was still serving out his sentence. Which is why your sister rushes home every night for a telephone call from a man she has never seen whom she met late one night on the telephone when he placed an overseas call for her to Nigeria. Which is why your mother pretended not to notice that your father was leaving her bedroom in the middle of the night for yours. Which is why your co-worker has started, despite your warnings, to take long coffee breaks with the biggest flirt in the office. Which is why you didn't say anything last night when he didn't put on the condom you'd placed on the night table.

When love and desperation are one in the same, it's called the Leah Syndrome.

[1] A book that helped to prompt my thinking on this matter and upon which many of the remarks here are based is Anne Wilson Schaef's *Escape from Intimacy: Untangling the "Love" Addictions: Sex, Romance, Relationships*, HarperCollins, 1989.

The Leah Syndrome

You know you're obsessed about a relationship when...

- You literally cannot get anything done because you're always thinking about him.
- You call his house or job and hang up when he answers the phone.
- You call his house and hang up when his wife or girlfriend answers the phone.
- You have failed to keep in touch with any of your friends, and when you do, virtually all of your conversation begins with, "He..."
- You drive by his house almost every day to see if his car is in the driveway.
- You schedule your day's activities around his telephone call — that is, when you're not sitting by the telephone waiting and waiting and waiting.
- You imagine that he's with another woman just because he is not with you.
- You'd do anything to get him to love you.
- You agree with him that whatever is wrong in the relationship is your fault — despite his erratic outbursts, his moodiness, his inconsiderate behavior, his negligence, and his put-downs.
- You'd rather die than live without him.
- You find yourself repeatedly giving in to his requests — even against your better judgment.
- You pull him close and then push him away at least seven times a week.
- You jeopardize your mental and physical health, your job, and your finances to please him.

- You are convinced that you can change him.
- You use the Bible and God to justify your actions.
- Each time the two of you make up, you are convinced that this time things will be better.
- You think you know him better than you know yourself.

It is called the Leah Syndrome.

I read Leah's story, and I think of the scores of women I know who love men who, for one reason or another, are incapable of returning their love.

Even so, to be involved with a man who doesn't love you is survivable. To be with one who hates you is another thing altogether. That kind of a relationship can crush you. You can live in dignity without love, but you cannot live with dignity with a man who hates you.

Rarely in my travels do I meet anyone from my past, and when I do, I admit that I am a bit nervous. It depends upon which part of my past I must reckon with.

One Sunday morning after I'd spoken, a striking woman came up to me in the church basement, shook my hand, introduced me to her two handsome children, and told me how proud she was of me. I was pleasantly surprised; I recognized Bonnie as soon as our eyes met. We'd been best friends when we were sophomores in high school. I was embarrassed that she'd had to wait in line for almost fifteen minutes to get my attention. All the warm memories rushed upon me as we laughed and held one another. How we'd loved to daydream and giggle together. She was still pretty, I thought – even if it was a sort of tired pretty now. I'd secretly envied Bonnie's good looks when we were teen-agers, along with the nice, quiet, peaceful, tidy home she lived in with her parents and brother. It was the exact opposite of the big, rambling, riotous, cluttered home I lived in with my parents and eleven sisters and brothers.

After exchanging phone numbers, Bonnie and I kissed and promised to call. Less than a week later, Bonnie kept her promise to call. I'm not sure I'm glad she did.

It seems that a few years after graduating from high school Bonnie married a man who, within six months of their marriage, was in jail for some unmentionable offense, leaving her pregnant and back home in her parent's household. He remained in jail for the first ten years or so of their marriage. During that time, Bonnie raised their son, joined her mother's church, worked hard, visited her husband virtually every month for those ten years, and remained celibate. Her husband was finally released, only to be sent back to jail within eighteen months for further offenses. This time when he went off to jail, he left Bonnie infected with some sexual disease that she couldn't bring herself to specify. And he left her again pregnant. By the time I saw Bonnie that morning in the church basement, she had, according to her testimony, prayed about it, forgiven her husband, and resumed the routine she knew best: She was working, living in her parent's house, visiting her husband every month in jail with their two children, attending church (a different one), and remaining faithful to her wedding vows. Bonnie ended her life's story with a rehearsal of verses from the Bible about submission, forgiveness, marriage, faithfulness, and love, which she explained served as the scriptural foundation for the decisions she'd made. Finally, she said, after much soul-searching, God had given her peace of mind. God had assured her that the next time her husband was released, their lives would be better.

It was now my turn to say something.

But what could I say? My friend had delicately woven a pious shawl of rationalizations with which to cover herself. There was just enough piety in her behavior to make one seem impious for challenging her. Did I dare tamper with the loose end that hung from her sheer garment of self-righteousness and risk unraveling what, no doubt, was raw pain? My degree in biblical studies and my ordination were no match for Bonnie's piety. I knew better than to argue Scripture with her. There was nothing in the Bible I could appeal to that she could not counter with other portions of the Bible. Besides, I reasoned, she didn't need the Bible; Bonnie needed a different god. For the life of me, I don't remember what I said. I am sure it was nothing intelligent, insightful, or interesting. I doubt I even came up with anything profoundly religious to say. I just remember wanting desperately to get off the telephone and get in the shower. Somewhere in me I felt stained.

Bonnie's story is Leah's story.

It wasn't until we hung up that I saw the pattern. It was too late to call Bonnie back.

Bonnie was living the only life she knew – her mother's life. From what I remember, when she wasn't working or cleaning her already-immaculate house, Bonnie's mother was always at church. She stood out among many of the mothers in the neighborhood as a woman who was clean, god-fearing, praying, proud, and aloof. She kept her husband's house spotless, his meals warm, and his sheets pressed – in case he came home. It seems that Bonnie's father's always had another place where he would from time to time lay his hat, so to speak. Bonnie, who looked just like her mother, was a typical teen-ager at fifteen: She smoked, wore make-up, and loved to dance. But when I saw my high school girlfriend almost twenty years later, she had become her mother: tired, but virtuous, and perpetually waiting. She knew less about living with a man and more about praying for a man whose depravity auspiciously became the kindling for her own righteousness.

Leah, too, was re-living her childhood. She was re-living in her marriage to Jacob her relationship with her father. That Laban had to trick Jacob into marrying his elder daughter says something about the father's opinion of his daughter. Of course, according to custom, the elder daughter married before the younger. And, of course, a case could be made that Laban was just looking out for his elder daughter. She was helpless, pitiable, and dependent. She was also unattractive (which was all the more damnable for a woman). According to the narrator, Leah's eyes were weak, meaning she lacked luster, beauty, charm, esteem – in the narrator's eyes, in her father's eyes, obviously in Jacob's eyes, and eventually in her own eyes. And judging from the way she allowed herself to be a pawn in her father's and Jacob's dealings, what her father (and Jacob) thought of her became what she thought of herself. But then Leah was a Hebrew woman, you say; she didn't know there was another way to see herself.

People addicted to relationships are quick to point out that what they are really looking for is intimacy. But what they really want is control, control over the other person. They want control over whether they will be loved (or related to) and how they will be loved (or related to). In fact, they go to great lengths to avoid intimacy. They pull you close and then they push you away. They want to be close without being accountable, or demanding accountability. They want the rewards of love without the pain of love. They want you to share your secrets without ever having to share their own. But to be intimate is to be dependent and to be depended upon. To be intimate is to know that you must have boundaries in order to remain whole. But to be intimate is also to be prepared to adjust those boundaries in order to recapture what sometimes gets lost in good relationships.

What makes it difficult to get through to someone like Bonnie (or Leah) is her belief that her suffering is redemptive. Her religion is her cape of captivity. It both chains her and protects her. It chains her to a life of abuse, and it protects her from having to take responsibility for her own life and happiness. She is waiting to be rescued, whether by God, by another relationship, or by a transformed husband. To rescue herself is to not trust God. She is afraid of being single and petrified of not having a relationship. Her "Jacob" is the scapegoat for her own disease. She organizes her life around his disease (e.g., sex addiction) and his faults (e.g., selfish, conniving). She would rather define herself as co-dependent than an addict.

That way, she can assign her affliction in relationship to someone else and not have to take responsibility for her own disease. Nor does she have to own up to her part in the sick relationship. She becomes the perfect sacrificial lamb: powerless, "blameless," dependent, but pious. To initiate her own deliverance is to preempt God. To make a decision is to lack faith in God. To save herself is to deem herself worth saving. To think of herself she must stop for the moment thinking about her relationship. To free herself is to not trust God to "save" him. Of course, she is his Messiah, and they are both waiting on God.

It is called the Leah Syndrome.

When is enough enough? Every woman has to decide this for herself. It took four sons and no change on her husband's part to convince Leah. One woman's waiting on God is another woman's "enough is enough." One woman's testimony about how God changed her husband is another woman's testimony about how God changed her. Some women prefer freedom to testimonies. And what was Leah's freedom? It was at least no longer beginning every sentence with, "Maybe now *he* . . ." It became, "This time *I* . . ." Whether she had to leave Jacob to find her own voice, we do not know. But eventually *it* came to her – with no intervention from her god or angels – it came to her. What is the "it" that came to Leah? Perhaps, "I don't want to live like this anymore." Perhaps, "I have a right to be happy." Perhaps, "I don't need to live this anymore." Perhaps, "I have a right to be free from being addicted to a man who hates me, free from being humiliated, free from being afraid."

And when it came to her, she stopped. Leah ceased bearing:

She ceased bearing Jacob's faults; she ceased bearing other people's opinions about her role as wife; she ceased bearing what she had been taught. She defined the problem, defined whose problem it was, and she stopped bearing other people's problems. Only then was she able to experience God for herself.

Eventually it came to Leah, and when it did, I imagine she said, "If you see my beloved Jacob, tell him I am through."

We only wish that Leah could have stuck to her resolve. But evidently she didn't. And that is another story altogether.

When Love Hurts

I seem unable to get away from stories about violence against women, whether they are biblical stories or contemporary stories. As soon as I think I can move on in my writings to other topics, I am drawn to another abused woman's story. I've never been physically abused. So why can't I let the topic go? Perhaps it is not my topic to let go of. Perhaps it has to let go of me. There are some issues that you choose. There are some issues that choose you. And the ones that choose you are like jealous lovers. They insert themselves into everything you do.

What new is there to say? I ask myself. Nothing, a voice answers. Just keep saying what has already been said. Perhaps this time some woman will hear you. A woman who asked for intimacy but settled for a black eye.

I have loved a number of men, but I have been *in love* with only two. The first man I fell in love with taught me how to receive love, and years later the second taught me how to let go of it. When the time came for me to move on from those relationships, I thought I would die from the pain. That's probably because I love like most women love — consummately. So when the second relationship ended, I walked around in a stupor for the first six months and slept almost all day, every day for the next six months. In the beginning I didn't know where to put all the love I still felt; later on, I didn't know where to put all the pain.

Many years have passed since I left the second man standing on a corner of Manhattan's east side, and the truth is that only recently has the hole in my chest begun to close. I suppose I first had to admit that love is rarely any better than the lover — that is, the deceptive love deceptively, cowards love cowardly, and fools love foolishly. For sure, the man in question loved me, but he loved me the way cowards tend to love. He loved me enough to tell me the things I wanted to hear, but not enough to tell me the things I needed to know. And foolishly, I stayed in the relationship a day too long. For I knew long before the day I walked away that I would *have* to walk away. But my feet refused to obey my good senses, and before I knew it, I had joined in the conspiracy of silence against me. So, I stayed. After all, I was as much in love with *being* in love as I was in love with him.

I first met the prophet Hosea's wife, Gomer, some years ago when I was searching for a dissertation topic. I couldn't understand why I had never noticed her before. I thought I knew most of the women in the Bible. But evidently I didn't. In truth, I didn't want to take her story on. I wasn't prepared to deal with a prophet's abuse of his wife. It was too complex, too controversial, and too close to home. I was still too grateful to the Bible for its healing stories to face its wounding stories.

Gomer's story is especially difficult to unravel because the author of the book made it virtually impossible to distinguish God's voice from her husband Hosea's voice. Hosea's demands, cajoles, threats, and acrimony against Gomer became virtually indistinguishable from God's demands of, pleas with, and threats against the land and people of Israel.

To lambaste Hosea was to lambaste God, I thought.

Before I walked away from my relationship, I learned that silence can be a form of violence between two people. When we refuse to confide, refuse to talk to one another, silence can be as savage as any fist to the face. By asking me to love him but insisting that I not query him, he was killing me – softly, subtly, but killing me, nevertheless. Fortunately, I left while I could still tell the difference between a caress and a strangle. But we all have different thresholds for pain. God knows mine is exceedingly low.

To be sure, love means exposing yourself to the risk of being hurt, deeply hurt, by someone you trust. You trust enough to lay down your armor, expose your scars, and divulge the secret of your sassiness. You trust that he will not laugh at what you show him or mishandle what you have given him. It is an enormous risk. At the same time, love involves risking the possibility that you might hurt the other person. Which, for some of us, is an equally painful thought. And because we are human, and as such are irreversibly imperfect, the chances are good that one day we will hurt and/or be hurt by those whom we love.

The task before us is to decide when hurt becomes torment and what to do when the torment exceeds the love. It may mean letting go of the tormentor – be it a lover, friend, or family member – and allowing the love to find another dwelling place. Evidently, this is a very difficult decision for some women to make. Some choose to remain in relationships long after the time that love has ceased to be just hurt – when it has become verbally, emotionally, or physically abusive; when kisses are interlaced with punches; when whispers of love are exchanged for threats of death. Perhaps you know this woman: She is your sister, your mother, your co-worker. Perhaps she is the woman in the mirror.

The story of Gomer haunts me. She was a woman victimized by Hosea, her husband, in the name of God. She was raped, brutalized, sexually humiliated, verbally assaulted, and threatened by Hosea. He repeatedly referred to her as a whore which, I suppose, was supposed to justify his behavior. But it didn't. It just made it all the more depraved.

This week I've received calls from two close friends who have chosen to remain with men who physically batter them. I've taken to my bed because each call leaves me more devastated than the one before. One is a college professor and the other a self-employed business woman. Though they differ in age, background, and personality, both are intelligent, attractive, ambitious, and talented. More importantly, my two friends share, tragically so, one more thing in common: Both are in love with men who beat them.

Gaye's[1] husband batters her like his father before him battered his mother. And when that is not enough, he threatens to kill her, their two sons, and himself. She believes him. I do, too. In the meantime, he

[1] The names have been changed.

disconnects the battery cable in her car and hides it, forcing her to walk the three miles to the restaurant that she owns and operates.

Toni,[1] the college professor, is married to a minister who chokes her and hurls the most vile and humiliating comments at her. And while she has left him more times than either of us can count, she cannot resist the husband who calls her all day on her job and all night at her sister's home pleading with her to come home. The man on the telephone is contrite, solicitous, and, according to him, helpless without her – so unlike the man a few days earlier who had thrown her clothes in the street. And because Toni's need to be needed is greater than her need not to be choked, she returns to a cycle of violence more vicious than the one before.

I am a minister, and working with women in the church has taught me that domestic violence cuts across class, race, and socio-economic lines: poor and rich women; black, white, Asian, and Latina women; the homemaker and the career woman; the passive and the aggressive woman; the religious and the secular woman – all of us are abusable. In fact, we all live in dangerously close proximity to it, wondering if this will be the time when he thinks that angry words are not enough. And the decision to stay in an abusive relationship is one that women from all different circumstances have been known to make.

Flesh against flesh. Flesh crashing against walls. Flesh falling to the floor. The sounds of screams and groaning in the middle of the night. I grew up with these sounds. When it was not coming from my own parents' room, it was the sound of Ms. Jeannette in the next apartment screaming for her life as her husband slammed her once more against the wall that adjoined our apartments. I could hear her children, my playmates, pleading with their father not to hit their mother any more. I'd lie in bed and promise God that if Mr. Johnnie would stop hitting Ms. Jeannette, I'd put all my Sunday School money in the offering plate instead of spending it on Mary Jane candy as I usually did.

Several times the only way Ms. Jeannette could escape her husband's drunken rage would be to dash out of the apartment without her blouse, never stopping to seek refuge in our apartment or any of the others in our complex. I guess she had learned some time ago that the women peering out the windows at her in the dark were too afraid to open their doors. To do so, they might have to admit that their own screams in the middle of the night had also been heard. And so they looked and wept.

That Gomer may not have been a real person — meaning that she might have been a symbol and metaphor for the people of Israel — seems, at least in some people's minds, to excuse the horror of the violence she was threatened with. In that case, Gomer was less a victim of violence than she was a victim of a metaphor. But metaphors can be as harmful as violence itself. Words hurt. Language from the pulpit that ignores women and silences the feminine cripples. It is amazing that god-fearing women have sat and listened to such talk for so long.

Women choose to remain with their batterers for various reasons, I suppose. Some of those reasons have to do with economics: She feels that she cannot, on her salary alone, meet the financial responsibilities of the house, the kids, or the lifestyle she has come to enjoy. So, she cannot afford to leave him. Some reasons are based on social factors: She doesn't want the children to grow up without their father in the home. A violent father is better than no father at all, she tells herself. Some reasons are physical: She prefers a busted lip to an empty bed. But, of course, these are the more obvious considerations.

There are others, less tangible and more subliminal, that have to do with secret fears and needs that make us lie to ourselves, turn our heads from the truth, and risk our lives for a false sense of security.

Admittedly, I don't always know exactly what makes my girlfriends stay with men who beat them, but I do know that one of the hardest things in the world is being a friend to a woman who stays in a relationship that is killing her.

The first time you ask her about her bruises, she gives you an excuse about having tripped over a toy. Even an infant could tell she is lying. The second time you ask her, she chuckles and says, "Oh girl, they're nothing. Eddie and I were playing, and he got a little rough." This time you sit in silence: Either she thinks you're crazy or you *are* crazy. By the third time, you pretend not to notice. After all, the first rule of friendship is never place your friend in a position where she has to lie to you. And the second rule of remaining friends with a battered woman is to conspire with her in pretending nothing is wrong.

Finally, you get a phone call, about half past two in the morning. She is sobbing and hysterical. She tells you the whole story: how he threw her down the steps and ripped up all her clothes; how the neighbors had to call the police; how he's just stormed out the door promising to return with a gun; how she can't take it anymore and is afraid for her life. By now you, too, are crying and your bedroom is spinning.

You offer to come get her, give her the name of a divorce lawyer, promise her money to get her on her feet, and threaten to send your brothers to bust his knee caps. She sounds convinced but asks you to give her a few days to pack. Three days pass, and you can't get in touch with her because her line is busy. You're worried sick, and you look a wreck. You've not slept because you've been calling, shopping, and rearranging the furniture in the spare bedroom. A week later you are sitting in a restaurant trying to pretend interest in your companion's conversation and in walks your girlfriend with her husband — the two of them hugging, grinning, and kissing.

She notices you and smiles sheepishly. She waves with her left hand; her right arm is in a cast. Is this a dream or are you crazy? Evidently, you're the only one in the room who's finished with him. Now, you're mad — at her and at yourself. You swear never to get involved again.

But that was before she calls you in the middle of the night the next week. And before you know it, you find yourself sucked back into the vicious cycle of violence and insanity, where he's physically abusing her, and she's emotionally abusing you. But you love your girlfriend. And your girlfriend is in love with someone who hits her for a living.

Judging by the story, to indict Hosea for sexual abuse was to indict God for sexual abuse. And I wasn't sure I wanted to take God on. But Gomer refused to be ignored that easily.

Of course, relationships go through seasons: seasons of misunderstanding, seasons of dis-ease, seasons of boredom, and seasons of tensions. And sometimes all it takes is that extra minute, that second chance, that holding on a little while longer to break the cycle. And provided there is some professional help, along with some honest admissions on both sides, even a tumultuous relationship can be healed. Without such measures, however, before we know it seasons can become lifestyles: Seasons of misunderstanding have become lifestyles of violence. And when that happens, something tragic follows. Like Gaye and Toni, eventually the woman begins to make room in her spirit for the violence. She braces herself for the slap. She plans her week around his anger. She no longer believes that she has a right not to be beaten.

And something even more perilous happens.

She ends up staying because she is no longer repulsed by the evil of the violence against her. She grows accustomed to making love with evil. She loves him. She makes excuses for him. She is bewitched by him. She protects him. She pities him. Like Toni, she lives for the moment of their reconciliation when he calls begging to be forgiven. That is when he is his most loving and attentive. More importantly, that's when he is at his weakest. For when he is weak, then she is strong. It is her one moment of power over him.

As grave as it is, however, physical violence is not the only way in which we hurt one another. It is just the most conspicuous. Nor are men the only ones in a relationship who inflict pain.

Men and women hurt each other. We hurt one another by lying to each other, by betraying one another's trust, by withholding important information from the other, by lashing out at one another, and by asking the other to do that which by nature he or she cannot do. Men hurt women. Women hurt men. Friends hurt friends.

It's true of me when I am too impulsive to stay and work things out, too frightened of relationships to give them a chance. Perhaps I have no idea what it takes to make a bad relationship better. After all, everyone makes mistakes, I tell myself; and sometimes people even change. Aren't those sermons that I've preached?

I have this recurring dream:

I am standing in the midst of a crowd. People are milling about. The mood of the crowd is restless, nervous. All attention is directed toward an area just beyond a gate several yards away. Eventually, a name I recognize is called. I look up. A silhouette of a man I once knew, a man

I loved, slowly makes his way through the crowd. I watch him, and a flood of memories I thought I'd forgotten rush over me. I still want to know why. I inch my way toward him. Maybe this time I can get him to look in my eyes. I speed up. I want to hear what he has to say. I begin to push. I press my way through the crowd. By now I am crying. I run. I press. When need be, I crawl. I must know why. Why did he lie? Why couldn't he tell me the truth? Why did he pretend as though he didn't notice the knife in my chest.

Finally, I am at the gate. His back is toward me. I reach for him. My nails dig into his shoulders. He turns and looks around. But the face that stares back at me is not his, but someone else's. It is the face of someone I'd betrayed a few days earlier, someone I'd left with tears in his eyes, the same tears I see now on his face. Something inside me bows. I close my eyes and whisper aloud, "Mercy."

I have never been hit by a man. Nor have I ever hit a man — though there have been times when I've wanted to. But, in my own way, I've hurt those who have loved me – as I have been hurt by those I have loved. In some cases, it was unavoidable. In others, it was wretched. And there have been times when I have just wanted to give up on it all. But we love, we hurt, we repent, and we learn. And we try again. Until we get it right-er. For our mistakes in love are what reminds us that we are human.

And despite my protests to the contrary, I know that when the time is right, I will plunge into love again. I can't help it: I was born to love. I like the way I think, feel, and look when I am in love, for then a great woman is transformed into a greater woman. And that's because my ability to love is what makes me less human and more like God.

When it was time for me to be done with grieving over the relationship I ended, I went out and bought myself a ring and placed it on the middle finger of my left hand. I called it my "I'm Gonna Live" ring. It was my way of celebrating my healing and commemorating my journey through brokenness. I needed something to remind me that life and happiness and wholeness and honesty are choices to be affirmed every day. I needed something on my finger to call attention to my hands, which I feel are one of the most sensuous parts of the body. Hands, I reasoned, are for holding and caressing, not striking and bruising. The truth was that I still loved him, or better yet, loved the memory of loving him. But if killing me with deceit was his idea of love, then I was willing and prepared to live without him. I guess you can say that I loved myself more than I loved the illusion of him loving me.

A Woman, a Well, and a Weakness

Oftentimes we look for intimacy in all the wrong places. Sometimes it is to be found in the strangest of places and with the most unlikely of people. Sometimes intimacy is different from what we imagined it would be. Sometimes it is in the meeting of two hearts. Sometimes it is in the meeting of two spirits. Sometimes it is in the meeting of two minds. Sometimes intimacy comes in the form of a conversation between perfect strangers. The relationship may not be a permanent one — nor does it have to be. But the experience of intimacy is a lasting one.

It began as an innocent conversation, of sorts. The stranger asked me for a drink of water. Recognizing by the horizontal stripping on both ends of his prayer shawl that he was a Jew, and by the slur of his dialect that he was Galilean, I asked why he, a Jew, ignored customs and presumed to talk to me. After all, I was a Samaritan and a woman. Such things were not done. Jews had no dealings with Samaritans. We were half-Jews, apostates of the faith, and mongrels of the race — or so the Jews believed. Besides, a pious man — whether Jew or Samaritan — would never have dealings with a strange woman. How could he tell whether or not she was menstruating?

The stranger, however, ignored my question about social customs and shifted the conversation instead to religion: *"If you only knew the gift of God . . ."*

I was accustomed to men: the way they manipulated conversations; the way they boasted with nothing in their hands; the way they promised gifts; the way they presumed so much about a woman after one innocent conversation, of sorts. I wondered what the stranger wanted. I studied him over my veil as I pulled my shawl tighter around me. Grateful that I could hide myself behind my veil, petticoat, linen dress, robe, and mid-body scarf, still I did not feel protected enough from the thoughts of this strange man. His dark, dark eyes seemed to look through me.

Still, his promise of water, *"living water"* he called it, was tantalizing. After all, water is a priceless treasure in this region of the world.

"Sir," I said, hoping to appeal to something decent in the stranger, *"where do you get this living water?"*

Even as I spoke, I felt myself being drawn into a conversation that one side of me wanted to end. I knew only too well that the best way to discourage strange men was to avoid answering them. If only I could keep the conversation on water and away from me. I wanted water. But I did not want the man. I wanted to avoid the side of him, the man, that promised women water but left them only disgrace.

Besides, what was this babble about water? I thought I knew every well between Judea and Galilee, surely every one in Samaria, some better than others, of course. And this one where we were standing was especially significant. Did this strange Jew presume to suggest that he had a well greater than the one even Jacob the patriarch had left for his people? Men are so arrogant, I thought. If he knew where better water could be found, why was he *here* pestering me for water?

The stranger did not answer my question, not directly anyway. Once more, he shifted the conversation, this time from religion to poetry: *"The water I give will become a spring of water welling up to eternal life."*

Was this his best line, or what? I wondered.

Why hadn't I simply followed my instincts and turned around when I saw the strange man sitting at the well in the middle of the afternoon. As though he were waiting for me. As though he knew I would come to draw water in the heat of the day. As though he knew I would do anything to avoid the whispers and reproach of respectable women who drew water in the cool of the mornings. Anything. I'd rather draw water in the heat of the day than subject myself to the insults of those pious women. They could be a scornful lot. Mine is a past and a present that drew more stares and gossip from pious women than water.

And what do you know: Today I'd carefully planned my trip to the well so that I might avoid the pious women in the village only to encounter a strange man with nothing in his hand, promising me water I would never have to draw again.

Still, the thought of never again having to make this long, back-breaking, lonesome trek to a well, never having to plan my day around avoiding the whispers of pious village women, never having to endure strangers sitting at wells with strange intentions – this was irresistible. As long as water was the only thing he was offering, I risked the request:

"Sir, give me this water so that I won't get thirsty and have to keep coming here to draw water." After all, ours was an innocent conversation, of sorts, I thought.

"Go, call your husband and come back."

I felt betrayed. How had the conversation gone from an innocent exchange about water to one about my husband? Why had I allowed myself to trust the strange man? Why had he taken the round about way to insult me? He knew that I couldn't accept a gift from a strange man without the consent of my husband. He manipulated me by exploiting my loneliness and thirst for water so he could expose me as a woman who'd married a number of men. How dare this strange man use my past against me!

"I have no husband," I responded abruptly. I reached for my water jar and got ready to leave. It was time to cut the conversation short. I refused to look at him. Besides, what business was it of his how many men I'd been with?

Oddly, the stranger did not seem to notice or mind the difference in my tone. Instead, he commended me for my bluntness: *"You have told the truth in saying 'I have no husband'; for you have had five husbands."*

I was not sure whether I should trust him. And I remained uncertain about his motives. Nevertheless, I was struck by the odd way the stranger commented on my lifestyle without condemning me:

"You have had five husbands, and he whom you now have is not your husband."

I stood for a moment peering at him from behind my veil. I

wasn't sure whether he could see the expression on my face. I was as curious as I was suspicious of him. One side of me wanted to run, while the other left me glued in my steps.

The stranger made no effort to take the matter of my husband any further. And neither did I. It was obvious that he was only interested in getting my attention. But how did he know about my comings and goings? He was a stranger and a Jew. Jews had no dealings with Samaritans. But this man was more than a Jew. He was a prophet man.

I knew a prophet when I saw one, and if not a prophet, then I surely knew a man when I saw one. And the stranger standing before me was both, of a different sort.

I stood there in the afternoon heat looking up at the scraggly bearded man with coarser-than-usual hair hanging down his shoulders, wondering what I should do. Should I leave or remain? Should I try changing the subject once more, or should I wait for his next remark? Should I risk hearing the details of my private life discussed by a stranger? But what did he know about my life? I wondered. What beyond the gossip of the viciously pious did he know about me? Nothing. He didn't know know anything about me. Hmmph, just like a man. One chance encounter with a woman, and he presumes to know her. No man knows me. Not even the men I've slept with. Just because they sleep with you doesn't mean they know you. Just because a man knows how to make a woman wrap her thighs around his waist and moan doesn't mean he knows what she's thinking when she slips out from under him and stares out the window in silence.

"... and he whom you now have is not your husband."

What did this stranger know? The man I now have is more my husband than the five men before him ever were: Benjamin, the one with the disease that left me barren; James, the one who left me because I was barren; Nicolaitus, who died a leper; Alexander, the drunk who beat me because I burned his food; and Simeone, who was executed because he was caught lying with another man's wife. Sure, I've lain with a number of men, but I have loved only one. And he was the one this stranger was claiming was not my husband. He would have been my husband were it not for the fact that he had run off to follow some prophet who promised him everlasting life. And I loved him enough to wait for him until he came to his senses.

But how do you make a man who has clearly never loved a woman know what it means to love? Don't ask me how I knew, but I knew: I knew the stranger didn't know anything about love. It was obvious there was no woman in his life. He was dusty and unkempt. He was serious and distant. He was coarse and blunt. Not to mention his gait. He lacked the swagger in his step that comes with having experienced passion and intimacy. More telling, however, were the stranger's eyes. Though his gaze was discomfiting, his eyes were a blank. It was as though he didn't even know what to look for in a woman. It was obvious that he'd been around women – after all, he was circumspect and respectful. But it was equally obvious that he'd never known one woman in particular. He knew how to stir a woman's soul, but I doubt whether he'd ever aroused a woman's heart.

This time, I decided to take control of the conversation. I decided to appeal to his ego. After all, he *was* a man.

"*Sir, I perceive that you are a prophet.*" Make a man think you're dumb and need his insight, and he won't notice that you've changed the subject, I thought. I put my water jug on my lap and leaned against the well. "*Our ancestors worshipped on this mountain, but you Jews claim that the appropriate place to worship is in Jerusalem.*"

He did not let me finish.

"*Woman, believe me . . .*" He spoke with such confidence, authority, and calm. "*The time is coming and now is . . .*"

90

I did not mind his interruption because something happened. It was as though the stranger was finally looking at me. But in a different sort of way.

"The true worshipers will worship the Creator in spirit and truth . . ." Then the strange man at the well began to talk to me, a woman, earnestly, patiently, about things no other man had ever spoken to me about: worship, the chasm between Jews and Samaritans, theology, the Spirit, the Eternal Creator, and the truth. It was if he had forgotten that I was a woman and a Samaritan. Or perhaps, he'd made me forget that he was a man and Jew. He spoke to my soul. But first he took seriously my mind. No man had ever spoken about such things to me. Without sounding esoteric or condescending, he talked as though he fully expected me to comprehend what he was saying.

"God is spirit, and whoever worships God must worship in spirit and truth." He did not presume that being a Samaritan or a woman would prevent me from grasping such weighty theological matters. He talked to me about things that prophets and rabbis talk to one another about, topics that occupy holy men. He talked about the coming of the Messiah.

"I know that the Messiah is coming, and when he does come, he will explain everything," I responded.

"I who speak to you am he." He said the words so matter-of-factly, I almost missed them. My mouth fell open. The Messiah? Could this man be the one? No, of course not. The possibility staggered me. But before I could say anything, men wearing striped shawls, talliths like the stranger's, joined us at the well. Judging by the way they positioned themselves around the stranger, they evidently knew him. They did not speak, yet there was no mistaking that they were surprised to find him talking to a Samaritan woman in public. Their gaze was fixed on me, and I lost my will or appetite to speak further. The looks on their faces

reminded me who I was in the eyes of the religious. These were the kinds of men I knew only too well. Their piety was much like my veil: While it covered some things, it hardly hid anything. They could hardly conceal their disdain for me.

I was glad, however, that what the stranger had given me in those brief moments even the petty imaginations of those around us could never take away.

To his credit, the stranger offered them no explanation for his behavior. Instead, he took the awkward silence as opportunity to drink from the cup I'd placed by his side earlier.

I readied myself once more to leave, although a million things raced in my mind to ask the stranger, things I had always wanted to know, answers to questions I'd spent my life searching in all the wrong places for. His friends had begun talking among themselves about food, the heat, the journey ahead, and others who'd gone on to make preparations. I resented their menacing glances in my direction. I resented more their intrusion into a revelation that had left me curious, though not yet satisfied. I decided to move on, however. For I was still a woman and a Samaritan. And he was still a man and a Jew. But what he gave me there at the well that afternoon sent me with my jug into the corridors of the town. This time, though, I wasn't searching for companionship. I was searching for those who were as desperate for water as I had been.

Just Friends

As a biblical scholar I am frequently asked my opinion on homosexuality. If I am lucky, I can avoid answering the question. Those who press for the biblical position on the matter rarely get a straightforward answer from me. For I know that it is rarely a biblical matter for the one inquiring. Of course, the more incorrigible do not wait for my insight. They come with their own arsenal of moral damnations.

But, as far as I am concerned, homosexuality is not simply a moral issue. It is an ethical issue as well. It is one thing to opine about morality or immorality in other people's choices. It is another thing to decide how to live with people whose choices are radically different from one's own.

While I must admit that my thinking on the topic is not always firm, my commitment to and love for my friends whose lives are different from mine is. I look at my friends and I don't see homosexuals, I see my friends. Just as I hope that they look at me and not see the woman who, when I survey my heart, I know myself to be: an impostor, a blasphemer, a moody woman, and one who holds grudges long past the season of forgiving. I hope they look beyond these things and see a friend.

We are all searching for intimacy.

"So how could you be friends with a lesbian?" a friend asked incredulously over the phone one evening.

"She's my friend because she's all the things I like in a friend," I responded calmly. "She loves being a Black woman; she has a demonstrated commitment to Black and other Third World people; she has a great sense of humor; and she's not fragile."

"Suppose she wants you to be her lover?" my friend inquired.

"Then she also has good taste."

To say that my friend on the phone, along with the vast majority of the Black community, is homophobic is simultaneously to understate and to oversimplify the issue. For, like all forms of fear and hatred, homophobia, which is the fear and hatred of people who love sexually members of their own gender, is irrational to the core. How do you explain a fear that makes people get up and leave when a gay or lesbian person sits down at the same lunchroom table? How do you explain a fear that makes students refuse to take a class from the English Lit professor because the rumor is she's a lesbian?

Charlotte was the first lesbian I ever met. Or did I ever really meet her? Come to think about it, we spent four years together on the same college campus, but we never really *met*. No one ever introduced us; and I don't remember ever talking to her – not really. What I knew about her being a lesbian was what I heard others say when she passed by in the library or walked into the dining room. I do remember clearly, however, that Charlotte was always alone. And while we, the sisters on campus, fancied ourselves to be far too well-bred and sophisticated to be rude, we did the next best violent thing: We ignored Charlotte.

So, what was – and is – it about lesbianism that frightens us? Well, we are afraid of what we don't know, for one thing. Sex is the one aspect of our being that we express the most, but know the least about. Very few of us ever become completely comfortable with our own bodies, even fewer of us ever become comfortable with our sexuality, and virtually none of us can explain why we get involved with the people we do. And we are threatened by those, in this case women, who are courageous enough to live their lives beyond what is construed as normal, and go on to love and make love with people who some consider to be totally inappropriate — whether their inappropriateness has to do with their color, their height, or their gender, to name a few. And to the extent that we hate lesbians, we hate them not because of what our fantasies tell us they do, but because they are different. And people who are different, we can't understand; and people we can't understand, we can't control; and what we can't control, we destroy.

I had grown older and had become less afraid of the things I didn't understand by the time I met up with Brenda in New York, where we were both struggling writers. Brenda was the second lesbian I met. I don't think Brenda ever flat out told me she was a lesbian — just as I never told her that I was not. I just knew — from her associations, from her writings, and from her genuine love for everything female. I remember the first time she invited me to her apartment to talk about an article I'd written, I was nervous and apprehensive. I don't know exactly what I thought she was going to do to me. That's not quite true: I wondered if she'd jump me and molest me the moment I stepped in the door. She didn't. She welcomed me into her home, showed me her dazzling collection of women's posters, served me a wickedly delicious cup of tea, and encouraged me in my writing. When it was time to go, I had to pass by her bedroom to get back to the front door; and I couldn't help wondering, imagining, thinking.

"I don't fear or hate lesbians; I'm just wildly curious about them," admitted one woman. I share her curiosity. And I suspect that, instead of fear and hate, curiosity is what most of the sane among us basically feel. A curiosity that we don't know how to inquire into, don't know how to articulate, so we hide behind lesbian-bashing. The real fascination about lesbians, for me, is that here is a population of women who do not share what is the abiding impulse of most other women in the world: the desire to please some man.

A lesbian woman wakes up and goes to bed every day and doesn't give a rip whether some man likes her hair, thinks she is overweight, likes her cooking, is angry that she was late, thinks her witty, finds her attractive. "Girls, how do you do it?" I want to ask. I equate their freedom with the freedom of people who go to bed and wake up every morning without ever having to worry about how they are going to pay this bill or that bill.

Though most straight women can't imagine what it's like not to be governed by the appetites of men, we do know how easy, how natural it is to love a woman. After all, the first woman we ever loved was our mother. How many times have I passionately hugged women friends I sorely missed, slept in bed with women friends because we were too afraid of sleeping alone, and cried bitterly when the woman I loved most decided she couldn't tolerate my friendship any longer. Strange, isn't it: Loving women feels easy and natural, but making love to another woman seems abnormal.

Common thinking on this matter was summed up by Deaconess Walker during Bible Study one Sunday morning when we were studying the story of Sodom and Gomorrah: "No disrespect intended, Rev, but from where I sit, it just ain't natural!"

But what is "natural" sex, Deaconess Walker? Sex between a male and a female, you say? Rape is sex between a man and a woman; is that *natural* sex? A nurse friend who works in the emergency room tells me that it isn't uncommon to see girl babies brought in for medical care because their little stomachs are full of semen or because their vaginas have been ripped apart by some grown man's penis. I ask you, is that natural sex? Ah, but you mean sex between two consenting adults, you say — male and female. But then you will want to legislate what *type* of sex between consenting, adult men and women is natural. Must it be one woman and one man, or can it be one woman and two men? The man on top or the woman on top? The sixty-nine position or the elusive Venus Butterfly? Vaginal only or will you permit oral sex, too? Must there be love for sex to be normal?

Will someone please tell me, what is *natural* sex? (Needless to say, Bible Study ended before we could pursue this discussion further.)

Deborah B. was my best friend when I was in the fourth grade. A day didn't pass when we couldn't be found in one another's company. We were each other's shadow or, more accurately, I was hers, since I was as dark as she was light. I always preferred her quiet, orderly home, which she and her sister shared with her divorced mother; and she preferred my rambunctious one because she had a mad crush on my older brother. Like Nel and Sula in Toni Morrison's second novel *Sula*, Deborah B. and I lived for one another, we loved one another, we stole for another, we lied for another, and, like the curious nine-year-olds we were, we learned about sex and sexuality by studying and exploring one another's body. We weren't lesbians, but girls together. Just girlfriends exploring the changing character of our pubescent bodies with someone we trusted.

After taking an informal survey of more than twenty-five heterosexual women who — like myself — are independent, out-spoken, hard-working, and hard-headed, I discovered, without exception, that all of us at sometime in our lives have been suspected, or openly accused, of being lesbian. Whether we were entrepreneurs, writers, teachers, secretaries, telephone operators, lawyers, labor mediators, store clerks, but especially if we were ministers; whether we were married, but especially if we were single, we were suspected of being lesbians. As one woman said, "I can usually tell how effective I am in my office when my sex life (or non-sex life) becomes the topic of conversation around the water cooler that day."

In light of the mindless homophobia (exacerbated by the hysteria surrounding AIDS) that exists in the Black community, the accusation of being a lesbian is most often a ploy to castrate a woman, to silence her, to scare her into obedience, to undermine her effectiveness before her peers and clients, and to remind her of her place. In some instances, it has been effective. For I've seen friendships terminated; I've seen women denounce other women to win male affection; and I've seen women turn in their placard and withdraw from a movement for fear of being labeled a lesbian. But then I've also seen heterosexual women embracing lesbian women in sisterhood, with no regard for who was looking, and marching together down mean streets on behalf of bereaved mothers in South Africa. And I've seen lesbian women raising funds for local battered-women shelters and woman-ing the phones all night at rape crisis centers.

Admittedly, my work as a writer and a minister often leaves me split at the root. As a writer, I explore the world of ideals, thoughts, emotions, words, and, being committed to the future, the truth. And as a writer, my natural peers are other writers. And because many, though not all, the male writers/artists sensitive enough to traffic in honest emotions are gay, and because many, though not all, the female writers/ artists sassy enough to tell the whole truth are lesbian, then many of my creative comrades are homosexual.

But, then, I am a minister in the Christian church. And, if you subscribe to the image of the popular, traditional, stereotypical Black preacher, then censuring people is my business — my only business. Part of my job, so goes the stereotype, is to determine who and what is right and wrong. And homosexuality has always been wrong according to the Black church and community. Hence, both personally and professionally, I am constantly called upon to choose between my instincts as a writer and my commitment as a Christian. And I've seen so many good people do the wrong thing for all the right reasons. Which explains why, for me, the most haunting passage in the Bible is the one where Jesus says, *"There will be those who will deliver you up to be killed thinking they are doing the will of God"* [1]

But, still, I would be less than honest if I didn't admit that I've had my questions and my doubts. Like, why didn't Deborah and I have a lesbian relationship? Is homosexuality a choice or is it congenital? What is it like to make love to a woman? Should lesbians raise sons? Of course, on the days when I am tired of living with integrity and tired of being a thinking person, the easiest thing is to condemn homosexuality. There are days when I've wanted to renounce my belief that a woman has the right to choose, the right not be discriminated against because of her choice of a sexual partner. And that belief is sorely tried when I meet lesbians I don't like, most of whom, I know, I wouldn't like were they heterosexual. And just as I resent men (and women) who try to silence me by calling me lesbian, so do I resent lesbians who decide on the correctness of my politics – and, therefore, my access to grants, publication, and office – based on my stand on homosexuality. But, I know that I must be able to separate distasteful personalities and politics from what remains fundamentally a righteous stand: a woman's right to love whoever finds her lovely. After all, I know what it's like to feel unloved. And I know what it is to be sent out, left out, and kept out because I am different.

I don't ever want to be guilty of inflicting upon anyone else that kind of torment. Nor would I want to be guilty of having silenced a

[1] John 16:2

poet like Alice Dunbar Nelson or a philosopher/poet like Audre Lorde (or a genius like James Baldwin) just because of who they sleep or don't sleep with. Which means, in the end, it isn't just a matter of what my stand is on lesbianism or heterosexuality. It is a matter of my stand on *people*, for behind those labels lurk real human beings, women with feelings, women with dreams, women who are more than their sexual preference. Women who deserve to be known and heard – like Charlotte.

A year ago I saw Brenda for the first time in more than ten years. We were attending a meeting of women writers and neither of us knew a soul there except one another. Because I tend to be shy around strangers, and she is far more outgoing than I am in such settings, I attached myself to Brenda and tagged behind her, meeting people she introduced me to and drinking gallons of store-bought water when I couldn't find anything to talk about. At night, in bed, when we weren't teasing each other about our bad feet and throwing pillows, we caught up on the whereabouts of former friends and talked about our next writing projects. I didn't ask her who Teresa was or when she first knew she was lesbian. Nor did she ask me why I never married or when I was going to grow up and use the word *lover*, instead of referring to the male species as *boy*friends. Perhaps, one day – when we are past the age of lust and lactation – we will ask. But, for then, it was enough for us to love and be friends with someone whose choice could never be our own.

On the last day of the conference, on one of those few occasions when I ventured to go off by myself – to the toilet – another woman who knew I was a minister, as well as writer, accosted me at the sink: "Oh, did you know that Brenda is a lesbian?"

"Hush your mouth, girl," I answered incredulously. "All this time, I just thought of her as my friend."

Sick and Tired
of Being Sick and Tired

Death is stalking me. I know it because I can't see as well as I did last year. I don't last as long in my exercise class as I did last year. I can see death casting its shadow over my body. The skin underneath my arms is softer. The moles on my face have grown bolder. Silver hair gathers at my temples. Illnesses drag on longer. Broken bones mend slower. Aches in my joints are more intense. At this age, every ache cannot be traced, every ailment cannot be remedied, and every loss cannot be regained. And I can't remember for the life of me which one of my offenses last year caused my next door neighbor to stop speaking to me. I guess this old earthly tent is decaying. And there is nothing I can do to prevent its decay.

The best I can do is try to manage the decay — to remain in, what for me, is the best of health; to exercise, eat right, and take time out for myself. It is not easy. But I try my best. I try to recognize the signs when my body's own natural decay is being accelerated by disease. It is frightening to realize, however, that I'm becoming that age when I increasingly find myself walking friends and loved ones through sickness and disease, and bidding some farewell to death. I cannot write my way out of death's hold on us. I don't know what the future holds. So I spend my days making the best choices I can about how I want to live out the the days I have allotted. I do not ask God for more time. Instead, I ask for what the elders call "a reasonable portion of health and strength." More importantly, I do not ask for riches. Rather, I ask for people in my life who will love me enough to comb my hair and wipe my mouth should the days come when I am no longer able to do either for myself. For my remaining days, I ask for intimacy.

———————————

—————————

"Renita, the lump is malignant." Claudette's words over the telephone that December evening sent me crumbling into the chair. "The doctor says it's cancer," she said.

It was my turn to speak, but I didn't trust the scream welling up inside to fully articulate my horror. Incoherent words swirled in my head: 'My girlfriend has cancer. Claudette has cancer. Claudette... cancer. Cancer... Claudette... cancer... cancer.' The words in my head did not sound right. They did not fit together. They made no sense to me. 'My girlfriend Claudette is too young to have cancer; I am too young to love someone with cancer. She is my girlfriend. Friends don't get cancer.'

My mind raced back to when Claudette first told me about the annoying, tender lump that was protruding just above her breast, how she asked me to feel it as we drove to the beach that afternoon, how we laughed at the sight of a lump almost as large as her tiny breasts. Oh, how we laughed and teased. Never thinking, never suspecting, never fearing that the lump we joked about was the lump that we had been warned about. It just couldn't be.

How long we held the telephone in silence, I don't know — Claudette sighing and me shaking my head. Maybe seconds, maybe minutes, but it felt like a lifetime. Long enough to see both our lives flash before us. "Girl, hush," I finally whispered.

"Yeah, girl," she said, grateful, no doubt, that the silence had been broken. And then we wept together.

Sickness and death had made their way into my intimate space. Mortality had come to introduce herself to me. And I wasn't prepared to meet her. I hadn't rehearsed my lines.

Claudette's cancer sent me reaching for my own breasts. It also got me thinking about women's health issues. It's impossible to turn on the television or read the paper without coming across some public discussion about the health care system in this country. The public rages, and rightly so, about the obscene rising cost of medical care and indignities suffered at the hands of profit-driven insurance companies. Sickness has become a luxury that only the affluent can afford. And illness has become a metaphor for the human predicament.

But in that one phone call, health and health care moved from part of the national conversation to a personal confrontation. I began to look at my body differently, more intently. I wanted to know more about my history with illness and my proclivity for disease. I wanted to know about my tolerance for illness. But when your mother is dead, a whole portfolio of information about you lies buried with her in her grave. For example, I have no one to remind me which childhood diseases I contracted. I can't remember how old I was when I was rushed to the hospital with appendicitis. I barely can remember when my menstrual cycle began . . . although I do remember my embarrassment as my mother stood over me in the bathroom. She watched as I followed her instruction how to fasten the sanitary napkin between my legs. I didn't want her to see me naked. I was embarrassed by my nakedness, as I was embarrassed by her nakedness – when I'd walk in on her changing her clothes or getting out of the bath tub.

Searching my medical history was my way of getting on speaking terms with death, but when my mother died, important parts of my medical history died with her. I had no way of finding out with certitude which diseases Baker women are susceptible to. What do we die of? I know several who have died of broken hearts. But my heart has mended when broken. My maternal grandmother died of a gunshot wound. But I don't know anyone with a gun. My mother died of alcohol-related illnesses. But I don't drink. My paternal grandmother died from TB, which my father insists was brought on by having too many babies in drafty, run-down shanty houses. But I rarely even catch a cold.

I can't for the life of me imagine what I am going to die from. Without my mother to offer me a sketch of what I might look like in old age, I am forced to invent my own images. A play song from my childhood comes to mind. Acting as the ringleader in a circle of girls, one girl yells out, "Aunt Dinah's dead," and the circle yells back, "Oh, how did she die?" The ringleader with her hands on her make-believe hips postures an adult woman's pose of sickness and exhaustion and replies, "Oh, she died like this." The circle studies her moves and mimes the girl's gestures as we repeated the refrain, "Oh, she died like this." Each refrain brings with it new affects of sickness and exhaustion, new images of what might have killed lovely Aunt Dinah. We were teaching each other how to die — like the metaphorical Aunt Dinah.

Claudette's cancer shook my world because she, like me, is under forty, a minister married to a minister, an ex-Pentecostal (whose implied theology is that sickness originates from one of two sources, the devil or God), and she is a woman from a family with no history of breast cancer. As for the latter, I've since learned with Claudette that eighty percent of the women who contract breast cancer have no family history with the disease. And equally staggering is the knowledge that breast cancer is now the leading cause of cancer deaths of black women. In fact, we are far more likely to die of breast, lung, cervical, and colorectal cancers because we are less likely to be diagnosed early. Black women tend to wait too late to be healed. We are uncomfortable touching our breasts. We clean our vaginas, but we do not examine the mouth of our vaginas. We do not know the signs of cervical disease. We do not heed the warnings of our bodies. By the time we finally get to the doctor, it is virtually too late to pray. Then we pray to God to do for us what we were too negligent to do for ourselves. And then we die, resigned that our premature death is the will of God.

Most of the women I know are sick, and they are tired. Including me. We are afflicted with cancer, high blood pressure, low blood pressure, migraine headaches, endometriosis, yeast infections, urinary tract infections, fibroid tumors, blocked arteries, decaying teeth, depression, lupus, multiple sclerosis, anemia, cataracts, AIDS. These are just the sicknesses that I *know* about. Yet, there are other illnesses that our insurance carriers do not recognize, alternative (albeit, experimental) treatment options for various diseases that they won't pay for, and diseases peculiar to Black women that very little research attention is devoted to.

We are sick, and our illnesses are compounded by our exhaustion. Exhausted from the demands and stress of working two or more jobs, from having to be mother, chauffeur, counselor, referee, cook, housekeeper, medicine woman, clairvoyant, and acrobatic lover. Superwoman. Oftentimes we are too exhausted to notice that we are sick. We are too tired to heed our bodies' warning that something is wrong. Deadly wrong. Some of us have no health insurance. Others of us work on jobs that don't give sick days. And those of us who do have sick days wind up taking them in order to stay at home with sick children because we work for companies that don't allow time off to care for sick children. Which means that once we have spent all our sick time caring for our sick children, sick mates, sick parents, we have no time left to care for our own sicknesses. It is an endless cycle. It is an endless circle of sickness and exhaustion. Who can afford to be sick? Who notices that she is sick? After a while, feeling sick and feeling tired feel the same. After a while, feeling sick feels *normal.*

There is something about trying to live healthy that smacks of self-indulgence. It feels selfish. To embark on an exercise regimen is to take time away from others and devote it to myself. To eat healthy and right is to insinuate that I have plans for my life. To close the door to everyone's demands and luxuriate in bath suds for thirty minutes is to announce that I have rights. I, like many women, have been socialized to believe that to be a woman is to be self-sacrificing.

Real women die from exhaustion. Real women are also modest. They are too modest to admit they are tired. Too modest to notice their bodies decaying. Too modest to caress their own breasts. Even if a woman does find the time to examine her breasts, how does she give herself permission to touch her breasts when, in this culture, touch smacks of masturbation? And how can she endure pap smears when touch reminds her of rape? And how can she admit to herself that she is at risk of contracting AIDS (which is ravaging the African-American female population across class lines) when she hasn't admitted to herself — because it would be a sin to be so — that she is a sexual being. Good religious women do not desire sex.

They say that the best treatment for breast cancer is early detection. But early detection requires routine self-examinations. And for a woman to examine her breasts, she must admit that she *has* breasts. And how do you teach a woman to examine and protect a body that she doesn't see as her own? How can she take responsibility for her health when all the cultural messages, from billboards and pop music to commercials and religion, are that she is property for other people's pleasures, fantasies, and rages; that she is a slave to her reproductive system; that she is imperfect the way she is; and that she must be content to be silent and invisible before her god?

Good health begins with healthy self-esteem. Wellness is a correlate to self-love. Assassinate a woman's ego, kidnap her spirit, take away her appetite for living, and you don't have to worry about her body. She will kill her ownself with food, with delayed medical attention, and with co-dependent, addicted relationships. A woman must feel as though she has a right to be healthy. She must feel as though life is worth living and that she has something to live for. Healing begins when she affirms with the late civil rights warrior Fannie Lou Hamer, "I'm sick and tired of being sick and tired." It's a shame that Mrs. Hamer wound up in 1977 dying of breast cancer. I wish she hadn't been so poor, so tired, and so beaten up by the struggle that she couldn't notice the lump in her breast, until it was too late. Did she care more for the rights of the Negro citizens of Mississippi than she did for her own health? Perhaps so. Why do women keep sacrificing their health and bodies for movements that overlook them?

The telephone interrupts my typing this chapter. It is Joan, a pastor, a student, a wife, and mother of three sons. Before I can tell her that I'm busy, she tells me the doctor's prognosis.

"She says that I am anemic, exhausted, and that I need to go somewhere and rest," Joan giggles.

"So, what are you going to do?" I ask.

"I'm going to pick up my sons from school, take them to their assorted ball practices and music lessons, go buy me some wallpaper, and then stay up tonight and write my final paper for the semester."

For weeks I avoided visiting my great-aunt who is more than ninety years old. I don't know this old and frail woman. She is no longer the proud, stiff-backed, agile, active, sassy matriarch of my family, the woman who went to work at sixty-two years old when she found out about social security. Today her gnarled body confines her to a bed in her granddaughter's home, her mouth agape, her eyes staring in space, and her body hooked to machines that monitor her decay. From time to time she grunts. She requires twenty-four hour care. She wears diapers. But evidently she isn't ready to die. She's been like this for several years now. It hurts me to see her this way. But I'm glad that I must. In this culture that celebrates youth and firmness, I need to be reminded that death is inescapably a part of what it means to be human. And dying is the final waltz of death.

When I took my three-month-old daughter to visit her great-great-aunt and sat her on the old woman's bed, the baby instinctively fastened her stubby fingers around her aunt's rubbery fingers as they lay limp on the bed sheets. The old woman weakly lifted her hand for the first time in years. Her mouth was still agape and her eyes remained empty. She sensed, I suppose, that there was no impatience, no duty, no plea in my daughter's touch. She knew that she had been touched by a baby and something in her responded. The angel of death was encamped all about my great-aunt, but even the angel paused in her vigil long enough to tip her sword to the angel of life swirling overhead.

In January, 1993, I received a telephone call asking me to participate in a memorial service for Audre Lorde, the warrior and poet who had died that November after a fourteen year battle with cancer. Audre Lorde had written considerably, candidly, prophetically about her battle with the disease, her battle with the racist, misogynistic, patriarchal medical culture that treated her, her battle to choose a treatment consonant with her politics, and her battle with her own fears. Cancer began in her breast and over the years metastasized to her lungs and elsewhere. It was a sad honor that was extended to me. I had been saddened to learn of Audre Lorde's death but was honored to be asked to liturgically express my feelings about a woman whose courageous words had inspired my own. Regrettably, I had to decline the offer. I was due to deliver my daughter about the time of the service. (As the goddess of poetry would have it, my daughter was born on the very day of the service.)

A few weeks after Claudette called me with news of her cancer, I sent her my copy of Audre Lorde's *Cancer Journals*. I wanted her to know that she was not alone in her fears and in her rage. Claudette and I had shared many of Audre Lorde's works back and forth over the years. When word came that the poet had died, I prayed that Claudette would not find out about it. But she did. I recall the poet's profound claim that our silences will not protect us.

The night before Claudette's surgery, six girlfriends from across the country organized a conference call to express in poetry, songs, prayers, and laughter how much we collectively and individually loved her. Each of us, for our own selfish reasons, wanted her to live. I wanted her to know how much I loved her as the big sister I always dreamed of.

"Do you want to see the scar?" she asked as we sat on her waterbed a week after her surgery.

I did not flinch and said, "Yes."

Inside, I was recoiling. Claudette opened her blouse, and my eyes followed the centipede across her chest and the catheter draining fluid from just underneath her arm down into a vial dangling between her legs. I was not repulsed by what I saw. In fact, I had to resist the urge to bend over and kiss the centipede. Months later, however, when she came to visit me, I didn't know how to touch what my eyes saw then. Months of chemotherapy had left my girlfriend bald and hyperpigmented. I wanted to cry. Looking at her hairless, charred body, a line from an ode to the self-sacrificing woman came to mind: "Charm is deceptive and beauty is fleeting, but a woman who fears God should be praised."[1]

I could see that Claudette was sick and tired, mad at God, and dazed by the chemo. I brought her home and put her to bed. When she talked of dying, I dared her to die. When she lamented her appearance, I handed her bobby pins and helped her with her wig. When she talked about being weak, I offered her my shoulder. When she talked about her anger at God, I taught her Pentecostal soul a few more choice curse words. I figure that anger is a healthy emotion: It'll keep you alive until your healing comes.

[1] Proverbs 31:30

Love will also keep you alive. Two weeks after my daughter's birth, I was rushed to the hospital with obstructed intestines. It seems that my guts were not settling properly after giving birth. I was nauseous, feverish, and bent over in excruciating pain. At first, I thought that the pain in my guts was a part of the postnatal experience. I didn't have a mother to tell me otherwise. Oftentimes the pain was so bad I thought I was going to die. Once, I thought about dying. Nevertheless, I wanted desperately to live to raise my daughter with whom I was falling in love daily. I also wanted to live because I loved myself. I loved my life. I loved my work. My life wasn't perfect, but it was worth fighting for. My healing began with saying, "God, I want to live."

There is a woman whose healing story is told in Luke.[2] She had been hemorrhaging for more than twelve years, and then she decided to take her healing into her own hands. She went to Jesus, but she did not bother reasoning with him. She did not ask his permission to be healed. She did not ask his disciples for an audience with him. She did not want to risk rejection. She did not want to reason with patriarchal objections to a woman's healing, perhaps. Perhaps she didn't want to risk losing any more blood and time to male fears of the mystery of women's bodies. She had paid out and prayed out. She was sick and tired, and she was sick and tired of bleeding. She was desperate to be healed. So the anonymous woman decided to sneak up on Jesus and take from him what she needed to be healed. The woman's courage and initiative brought her to Jesus' attention. He confessed that it was more her virtue than his own that gave her back her life: "Woman, your faith has healed you." Was it her faith in Jesus, or was it her faith in her right to live whole that he commended? Perhaps both.

[2] Luke 8

"Tell your readers that my cancer was diagnosed as 'aggressive and virulent,' " Claudette instructs me when I ask her permission to recount her story. She is singing an old Pentecostal song that we both grew up with. I type the diagnosis with dread. Her hair has grown back more beautiful than before. Her skin is glowing. In the background to my typing, she is curling her hair with her hair irons and dancing in my bathroom. Before I let her read portions of this chapter, I show her pictures of my daughter's birth and try to describe for her the indescribable pain of giving birth to a child. She listens intently.

"It is not unrelenting pain, as I had imagined," I begin. "In fact, within its one minute duration — at every three minute intervals — labor is a dance with death."

"Is it true as the Bible says that you forget the pain?" she queried, studying the pictures.

"That's a lie from the vain imaginations of some man," I answer.

Claudette reads a portion of this chapter and begins to weep. "Just when I think I've healed from the emotional wounds that cancer brings," she says, "something comes along to remind me that this is a wound that never heals."

I cry with her. Not being the demonstrative one, I fumble as I reach out to embrace my girlfriend. We weep on each other's shoulder. "I want you to live," I whisper in her ear.

"I want to live," Claudette whispers back.

The stakes have changed. Instead of girls teaching each other how to die, we are women fighting to live.

Bibliography

The following is a partial list of books that provoked me, inspired me, and stretched my thinking as I was writing and contemplating writing *I ASKED FOR INTIMACY*:

Allender, Dan B. *The Wounded Heart: Hope for Adult Victims of Childhood Sexual Abuse.* Colorado Springs, CO: NavPress, 1990.

Beattie, Melody. *Codependent No More.* San Francisco: Harper/Hazelden Books, 1987.

Bell-Scott, Patricia, et al. *Double-Stitch: Black Women Write About Mothers and Daughters.* Boston: Beacon Press, 1991.

Bepko, Claudia, ed. *Feminism and Addiction.* Binghamton, NY: The Haworth Press, 1991.

Berry, Carmen Renee. *When Helping You is Hurting Me: Escaping the Messiah Trap.* New York: HarperCollins, 1989.

Bishop, Jim. *The Day Christ Died.* New York: HarperCollins, 1957, 1977, 1991.

Bryant, Cecilia Williams. *Kiamsha: A Spiritual Discipline for African American Women*. Baltimore, MD: Akousua Visions, 1991.

Darr, Katheryn Pfisterer. *Far More Precious than Jewels: Perspectives on Biblical Women*. Louisville, KY: Westminster/John Knox Press, 1991.

Edelman, Marian Wright. *The Measure of Our Success: A Letter to My Children and Yours*. Boston: Beacon Press, 1992.

Fiorenza, Elisabeth Schussler. *But She Said: Feminist Practices of Biblical Interpretation*. Boston: Beacon Press, 1992.

Hooks, Bell. *Talking Back: Thinking Feminist, Thinking Black*. Boston: South End Press, 1989.

Kubetin, Cynthia, and James Mallory, M.D. *Beyond the Darkness: Healing for Victims of Sexual Abuse*. Houston, TX: Word/Rapha Publishing, 1992.

L'Engle, Madeleine. *A Circle of Quiet*. New York: Farrar, Straus, & Giroux, 1971; New York: HarperCollins, 1977, 1984.

Lorde, Audre. *The Cancer Journals*. San Francisco: Aunt Lute Books, 1980.

Mason, Mike. *The Mystery of Marriage: As Iron Sharpens Iron*. Portland, OR: Multnomah, 1985.

Merton, Thomas. *Bread in the Wilderness*. Collegeville, MN/Philadelphia, PA: The Liturgical Press/Fortress Press, 1953, 1986.

Rank, Maureen. *Dealing with the Dad of Your Past*. Minneapolis, MN: Bethany House, 1990.

Rubin, Lillian B. *Intimate Strangers: Men & Women Together*. New York: HarperCollins, 1984.

Schaef, Anne Wilson. *Escape From Intimacy: Untangling the "Love" Addictions*. New York: HarperCollins, 1990.

Tannen, Deborah. *You Just Don't Understand: Women and Men in Conversation*. New York: William & Morrow Co., 1990; Ballantine, 1991.

Weems, Renita J. *Just A Sister Away: A Womanist Vision of Women's Relationships in the Bible.* San Diego: LuraMedia, 1988.

White, Evelyn C. *Chain Chain Change: For Black Women Dealing with Physical and Emotional Abuse.* Seattle, WA: Seal Press, 1985.

White, Evelyn C., ed. *The Black Women's Health Book: Speaking for Ourselves.* Seattle, WA: Seal Press, 1990.

Photo: Bill Hughes

RENITA J. WEEMS is an Assistant Professor in Old Testament Studies at Vanderbilt University Divinity School and an ordained elder in the African Methodist Episcopal Church. A former economist, public accountant, and stockbroker, she is both a scholar and a writer. In addition to her scholarly works in the area of Old Testament Studies, she has also published numerous articles in ESSENCE, MS, and SAGE. Her teaching and writing continues to expand as she travels across the country, speaking, preaching, and leading seminars. She lives with her husband, Martin Espinosa, and her daughter, Savannah, in Nashville, Tennessee.

Other LuraMedia Publications

BANKSON, MARJORY ZOET

Braided Streams:
Esther and a Woman's Way of Growing

Seasons of Friendship:
Naomi and Ruth as a Pattern

"This Is My Body. . .":
Creativity, Clay, and Change

BORTON, JOAN

Drawing from the Women's Well: *Reflections on the Life Passage of Menopause*

CARTLEDGE-HAYES, MARY

To Love Delilah:
Claiming the Women of the Bible

DARIAN, SHEA

Seven Times the Sun:
Guiding Your Child through the Rhythms of the Day

DOHERTY, DOROTHY ALBRACHT and McNAMARA, MARY COLGAN

Out of the Skin Into the Soul:
The Art of Aging

DUERK, JUDITH

Circle of Stones:
Woman's Journey to Herself

I Sit Listening to the Wind:
Woman's Encounter within Herself

GOODSON, WILLIAM (with Dale J.)

Re-Souled: *Spiritual Awakenings of a Psychiatrist and his Patient in Alcohol Recovery*

HAGEN, JUNE STEFFENSEN, Editor

Rattling Those Dry Bones:
Women Changing the Church

JEVNE, RONNA FAY

It All Begins With Hope:
Patients, Caretakers, and the Bereaved Speak Out

The Voice of Hope:
Heard Across the Heart of Life

with ALEXANDER LEVITAN
No Time for Nonsense:
Getting Well Against the Odds

KEIFFER, ANN

Gift of the Dark Angel: *A Woman's Journey through Depression toward Wholeness*

LAIR, CYNTHIA

Feeding the Whole Family: *Down-to-Earth Cookbook and Whole Foods Guide*

LODER, TED

Eavesdropping on the Echoes:
Voices from the Old Testament

Guerrillas of Grace:
Prayers for the Battle

Tracks in the Straw:
Tales Spun from the Manger

Wrestling the Light:
Ache and Awe in the Human-Divine Struggle

MEYER, RICHARD C.

One Anothering: *Biblical Building Blocks for Small Groups*

MODJESKA, LEE

Keeper of the Night: *A Portrait of Life in the Shadow of Death*

NELSON, G. LYNN

Writing and Being: *Taking Back Our Lives through the Power of Language*

O'HALLORAN, SUSAN and DELATTRE, SUSAN

The Woman Who Lost Her Heart:
A Tale of Reawakening

PRICE, H.H.

Blackberry Season:
A Time to Mourn, A Time to Heal

RAFFA, JEAN BENEDICT

The Bridge to Wholeness:
A Feminine Alternative to the Hero Myth

Dream Theatres of the Soul:
Empowering the Feminine through Jungian Dreamwork

ROTHLUEBBER, FRANCIS

Nobody Owns Me: *A Celibate Woman Discovers her Sexual Power*

RUPP, JOYCE

The Star in My Heart:
Experiencing Sophia, Inner Wisdom

THOMPSON, G. F.

Slow Miracles: *Urban Women Fighting for Liberation*

WEEMS, RENITA J.

I Asked for Intimacy: *Stories of Blessings, Betrayals, and Birthings*

Just a Sister Away: *A Womanist Vision of Women's Relationships in the Bible*

LuraMedia, Inc.
7060 Miramar Rd., Suite 104
San Diego, CA 92121

LURAMEDIA™

Books for Healing and Hope,
Balance and Justice
Call 1-800-FOR-LURA for information.